The History of the English House

SHELDONS, WILTSHIRE.

The History of the English House

From early feudal times to the close of the eighteenth century

J. Alfred Gotch

MA, FSA, RIBA

Bracken Books
LONDON

Previously published as *The Growth of the English House*
by B. T. Batsford, London, 1909.

This edition published 1985 by Bracken Books,
a division of Bestseller Publications Ltd.
Brent House, 24 Friern Park, North Finchley,
London N12, England.

ISBN 0 946495 75 0

Printed and bound in the German Democratic Republic by Zimex.

PREFACE.

THE object aimed at in the following pages is to tell the story of the growth of the English house from its first appearance in a permanent form down to the time of our grandfathers, when it lost much of its interest. Although it is a history of domestic architecture, no deep architectural knowledge is required to understand it; technical terms are avoided as far as may be, and of such as are used a glossary will be found at the end of the volume. The reader unacquainted with architecture will be able to follow the story without difficulty; but he who already knows something of our English buildings will of course be better able to link it up with the general development of English architecture. It is the main stream of progress which is followed, but there are many pleasant backwaters and interesting tributaries which it is impossible to explore in the space at command. Those who are desirous of pursuing the subject more minutely will have no difficulty in finding books dealing with particular periods—Mediæval, Tudor, Early Renaissance, or Late Renaissance. Hitherto, however, the panorama has not been unrolled from end to end in one volume.

To render the subject intelligible numerous illustrations are essential, and thanks are due to all who have kindly contributed in this respect, especially to the publishers, Messrs Batsford, whose assistance in this and other respects has been invaluable. In view of the many admirable books which appear from year to year, it becomes increasingly difficult to avoid familiar ground; indeed the mediæval period presents very few fine examples which have not at one time or another been figured. The reader is therefore requested not to be impatient if he meets with a number of old friends in the early part of the book, and to be equally considerate if, in the periods where examples are more abundant, he misses some of the best-known houses, inasmuch as the aim has been, so far as was compatible with the proper treatment of the subject, to illustrate the text with un-familiar buildings.

In order not to distract attention, footnotes and references have been avoided, and with a view to help those who are not conversant with the subject, there will be found, in addition to the short glossary, a chronological list of the principal buildings tabulated under the reigns of the English monarchs.

J. A. G.

WEEKLEY RISE, *near* KETTERING,
September 1909.

CONTENTS.

CONTENTS.

Norham Castle, Northumberland.

CHAPTER I.

INTRODUCTORY—THE NORMAN KEEP.

THOSE who, in the course of their wanderings through the remote districts of England, whether on business or on pleasure bent, have seen the lonely tower on the hillside, or the grey ruins of some ancient dwelling gleaming through the spaces of encircling trees, have no doubt often speculated as to the precise significance of these remnants of antiquity. They may have dismissed them from consideration as being relics of a past order of things having no connection with the concerns of the present day. Yet to the dweller in a modern house these maimed survivals have as much interest as have his own ancestors; and the home to which he returns after his travels can trace its descent step by step from those rugged masses of stone which roused his interest as he passed them by.

It is not difficult for any one to trace a likeness between the house of to-day and that of, let us say, the time of Elizabeth; but the resemblance between an Elizabethan manor house and a Norman castle or a Northumbrian peel-tower is not by any means so obvious, yet the descent of one from the other can be clearly

A

established. It is the object of the following pages not only to show how this can be done, but to trace briefly the continuous changes which have transformed, in the course of some seven or eight centuries, the gaunt and desolate keep into the comfortable mansion or villa of our own experience.

Everybody knows that an Englishman's house is his castle, but it should also be remembered that in early times an Englishman's castle was his house. Castles were not necessarily military strongholds; many of them were so, but many of them, again, were nothing more than fortified houses, and it is in these fortified houses that we must seek the first germs of our own homes, the earliest evidences of domestic architecture.

In this inquiry we need not trouble ourselves about Roman villas; they were exotic, and there is no reason to believe that they had any influence on English houses. Nor need we spend much time on the centuries which elapsed between the extinction of the Roman civilisation and the Norman Conquest. The country was widely populated during those years, but any one who has climbed the bleak downs whereon its inhabitants clustered, or scrambled up the vast earthworks which were the strongholds of its chieftains, may well wonder how the race survived. Some kind of shelter from the weather there must have been, probably in the shape of wooden buildings. But such primitive structures cannot be considered as architecture, and we will now concern ourselves only with buildings of a permanent nature on which a certain amount of trained skill has been bestowed, buildings, in fact, which convey definite information as to their arrangement, and may be classed, more or less, as works of art. Such buildings—at any rate so far as they are dwellings—are not to be found of a date prior to the Conquest, nor, with few exceptions, for more than half a century later.

The "castles" of the Conqueror were probably merely the huge earthworks which he found scattered throughout the land. Any new works which he caused to be made were probably of wood. It was not until the middle of the twelfth century that stone buildings superseded to any great extent these wooden structures ; at least few existing remains can be dated earlier than then ; and it is in the midst of the great ditches of these earthen "castles" that many of the stone keeps of that time were built, the encircling outer mounds being further strengthened by stone walls.

The few remains of the stone castles built during the reigns of the Conqueror and his sons do not provide us with any definite link between themselves and their pre-decessors of wood, although it is probable that they embodied in a permanent form the kind of accommoda-tion previously provided in more perishable materials ; the most important part of this accommodation being the hall. They certainly do not seem to have had any long ancestry on the other side of the Channel, for it is doubtful whether any building of this nature in Normandy can be dated prior to the Conquest. But although the exact causes which determined their shape are still to seek, it is clear that the fashion became established of erecting stone castles, wherein the keep was the principal building.

The keep was the domestic part of the castle ; it contained the rooms used by the owner and his family. Surrounding it at some distance was the outer wall strengthened according to circumstances by projecting towers and entered through a fortified gatehouse. The extent and intricacy of the defences varied according to the importance of the castle ; but these matters belong rather to military architecture than to domestic, and all that need be said is that those retainers who overflowed from the towers and other permanent buildings were housed in temporary wooden buildings within the court-yard.

Wooden buildings were indeed the ordinary dwellings of the time. There must have been many more people outside than inside the castles, even if we regard the castles which have survived as only a small part of those which actually existed. The ordinary manor houses, as well as the homes of the peasantry, were built of wood and have in consequence entirely disappeared. It is true that there are many wooden houses (or houses of wood and plaster) still to be found in all parts of England, but they are all of a much later date. It is doubtful if a single specimen of the twelfth century survives. It must also be remembered that not infrequently the inferior rooms of a stone house, such as the kitchen, were built of wood.

The keep, then, is the earliest form of English house built in permanent fashion. It was not, as some suppose, a prison or dungeon, or even the last refuge of a beleaguered garrison; it was the ordinary home of the family. In examining the ruins of a castle where the keep is the principal remnant, it is not necessary to postulate a vast array of other buildings, and to wonder what they were, and whither they have disappeared. It was probably the only considerable building, the remainder of the establishment consisting of a wall of enclosure and various minor buildings, mostly of wood.

What, then, was the accommodation in these keeps, these homes of our ancestors of the twelfth century, of the men who slew Thomas à Becket, of the barons who revolted against Henry II.?

The keeps were massive rectangular structures several storeys in height, with walls of great thickness. Their size varied according to the requirements of the owner. Some were about 90 ft. square, others but 30 or 40 ft. They were not necessarily exactly square, but, as a rule, their sides were of nearly equal length. The White Tower of the Tower of London, begun by order of the Conqueror in the later years of the eleventh century, measures 118 by 107 ft. The keep of Rochester Castle, built about 1130, is 70 ft. square. Castle Hedingham in Essex, built about the same time, is 60 by 55 ft.; the keep of Dover Castle (about 1154) is 90 ft. square; Castle Rising (Fig. 1), probably a few years later in

1. Castle Rising, Norfolk. The Keep.

date, is 75 by 60 ft.; Kenilworth, dating from the third quarter of the century, is 87 by 54 ft.; while the Peak Castle in Derbyshire, erected about 1176, measures some 40 by 36 ft. These are all outside measurements, and as the walls were very thick, seldom less than 8 ft., and sometimes as much as 16 or 20 ft., the available space within them was much less than their total area. Nevertheless, after deducting the thickness of the walls, there remained in the largest such huge rooms as that in the

Tower of London, 90 ft. long by 37 ft. wide; in the medium-sized, such as Hedingham, rooms 38 by 31 ft.; while in the smallest, such as the Peak Castle, the space was 22 by 19 ft., equal to the drawing-room of an ordinary house of the present day. But although the rooms were spacious, they were few in number, and badly lighted. As a rule there was but one room on each floor; some of the more important, however, such as Rochester and Castle Rising, had two large rooms on each floor and one or two smaller, but this was the exception rather than the rule. Occasionally a chapel was added; sometimes it occupied part of the floor space inside the walls; sometimes, as at Conings-burgh, it was contrived within the thickness of the wall itself, augmented by hollowing out one of the huge buttresses. But the chapel was always small—space was too valuable for it to be otherwise; and it was used not only for sacred purposes, but also not infrequently as a private room for the lord.

There are many examples of Norman keeps remaining in various parts of the country, but it will be sufficient to describe two of them as being typical of their fellows. One, although not of the largest size, was yet a fine building; it is Hedingham Castle in Essex: the other is small, the Peak Castle in Derbyshire. The former is among the very few of existing keeps that can be dated earlier than the reign of Henry II. who came to the throne in 1154. The chaotic times of his predecessor, Stephen, saw the erection of many castles which became the scenes of frightful oppression and outrage; but after his death they were razed to the ground, and apparently with great thoroughness, since no examples, it may be said, are to be found which can be safely dated between the years 1135 and 1154, during which period he nominally reigned over England.

CHAPTER II.

THE KEEP DESCRIBED.

THE great keep at Castle Hedingham is a fine specimen of the work of the twelfth century. Its exact date has not been ascertained, but its arrangement and its architectural detail point to the same date as Rochester Castle (about 1130), and good authorities go so far as to suggest that the same designer was employed on both. It has all the characteristics of an early keep; a vast, plain mass of masonry, slightly broken by the long vertical lines of shallow buttresses and angle turrets, and pierced at each floor with small windows—smallest near the ground where most accessible (Fig. 2). The entrance, as at Peak Castle, and all early keeps, is some feet above the ground, and in this case is approached by a flight of steps; it leads into the first floor, below which at the ground level, or thereabouts, is the cellar or store-room, approached only from the room above it. The plan is quite simple (Fig. 3), consisting of a large room (38 by 31 ft.) on each floor, enclosed by thick walls which are honeycombed with mural chambers and recesses. Some of these chambers are *garde-robes*, others were no doubt used as sleeping places by the family and principal guests. Over the entrance floor were two others; first the hall, a room with two tiers of windows, the upper of which gave on to a gallery or triforium which made the circuit of the building in the thickness of the wall: above the hall another room very similar to that on the entrance floor.

Then came the roof, round which was a rampart walk protected by the battlements, and leading to the four angle turrets which rose above the general mass of the building. Access to these various floors was given by a commodious circular staircase more than 11 ft. in

2. Castle Hedingham, Essex.   The Keep (*cir.* 1130).

The head of the entrance door is visible on the left :
the opening on the right is modern.

diameter.   There were thus four main rooms ; the basement, the entrance floor, the hall of two storeys, and the room over it. All these, except the basement, were warmed by a large fireplace, and lighted—if lighted it can be called—by eight small windows. The hall had in addition eight two-light windows in the triforium.

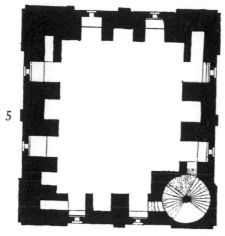

FOURTH FLOOR PLAN

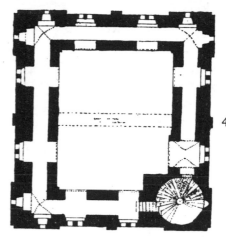

THIRD FLOOR (GALLERY) PLAN.

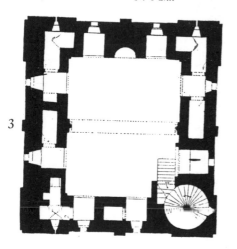

SECOND FLOOR PLAN (AUDIENCE HALL)

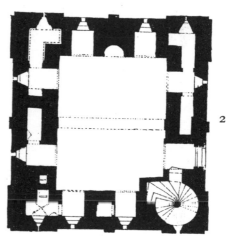

FIRST FLOOR PLAN (ENTRANCE)

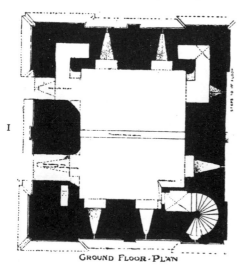

GROUND FLOOR PLAN

3. Castle Hedingham, Essex.

Plans of the Keep.

1. Ground Floor, or Basement.
2. First, or Entrance Floor.
3. The Great Hall.
4. Upper part of Hall, with Gallery.
5. Room over Hall.

SCALE OF 0 5 10 20 FEET

There is no room which can be identified as the kitchen ; there is no indication that the windows were glazed.

Against the means of attack which were then available this place was impregnable, but the safety thus assured must have been both gloomy and draughty. In its way, however, it was a lordly residence ; the main rooms were spacious, the smaller rooms were considerable in number, the staircase was of ample width. The gallery must have afforded a certain amount of quasi-privacy to those who were not privileged to occupy the mural chambers. The architectural detail of the doorways, windows, arches, and fireplaces is good (Figs. 4, 5, 6).

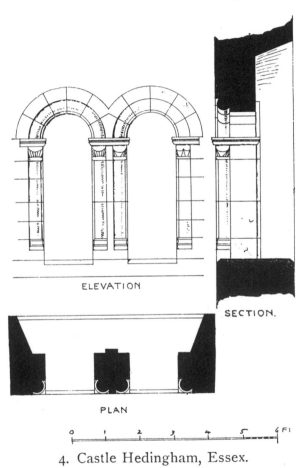

ELEVATION

SECTION.

PLAN

4. Castle Hedingham, Essex.

A window of the gallery in the hall.

Across the middle of the entrance floor and of the hall is thrown a fine bold semicircular arch, of nearly 30 ft. span, to carry the floor of the room over (see section, Fig. 5) ; the whole treatment is simple, sturdy, and splendid, as befitted the chief stronghold of

SCALE OF | 10 | 5 | 0 | 10 | 20 FEET

5. Castle Hedingham, Essex.

Section of the Keep.

the race for whom it was built, the De Veres, Earls of Oxford.

The fireplaces had not a flue such as we understand it, that is a long shaft running up the whole height of the building and crowned by a chimney; instead of this they had a short funnel contrived in the wall, and leading almost directly to small vertical openings in the

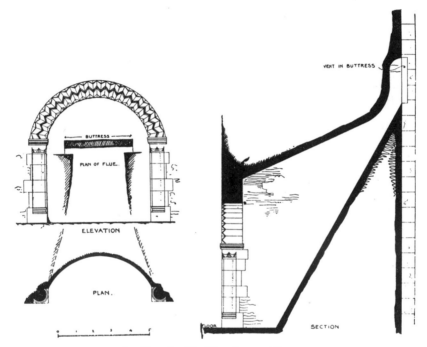

6. Castle Hedingham, Essex.

A Fireplace.   Showing the short flue leading to a vertical vent in the face of the wall.

face of the wall, cleverly concealed in the angle of a buttress (Fig. 6). The fireplaces, moreover, were mere recesses in the wall surmounted by round arches; there was no attempt at a projecting hood or any such ornamental feature as we are accustomed to think of as a chimney-piece. These things were to come later. They were, however, of generous size, as indeed they might well be, for it must be remembered that the windows were not glazed, and although they were too small to make the place cheerful, they were quite large enough to make it cold, and as each side of the room had an outside wall, the wind, from whatever quarter it blew, would find its way in. It is true that there were wooden shutters to the windows, which could be shut at night, but in spite of this there was every inducement to maintain a large fire; the volume of the flame may have overcome the disadvantage of the short flue, but the smoke must have had difficulty in escaping through the small vents, and doubtless much of it eventually found its way out through the open windows.

The sleeping accommodation was very meagre. The lord, and perhaps some of his family, had separate retiring places; they could not be called rooms, for they were only such chambers as could be contrived in the thickness of the walls; and in point of size, although not at all in point of luxury, were comparable to a sleeping compartment on a modern *train de luxe*. The household, men and women, old and young, slept in the great hall, a custom which conduced neither to comfort nor the observance of the proprieties. In the same room the whole establishment had its meals. During the greater part of the day the men, at any rate, were occupied with outdoor pursuits.

The Peak Castle, at Castleton in Derbyshire (Fig. 10, p. 19), is an extremely interesting example of an early dwelling. Its situation may be described as highly romantic, although that adjective of course expresses a sentiment which is of comparatively modern origin. Up to about the middle of the eighteenth century, travellers regarded such desolate places as Old Sarum, or ruins so difficult of access as the Peak Castle, with feelings approaching to horror. It was only towards the end of that century, or in the early years of the nineteenth, that the romantic aspect was appreciated.   It is tolerably certain that romance had no part in the selection of this site for a dwelling, but rather the assurance of security which it offered.   An extremely steep spur of the rocky hill which forms one side of a precipitous dale—one of the dales for which Derbyshire is famous—is deeply bitten into by a gorge which almost severs it from its parent ridge (Fig. 7).   An irregular triangle of rocky ground is thus formed rising steeply from its longest side up to the opposite angle, and bounded on one side by the precipitous slope of the dale, and on the other by the sheer descent of the gorge.   No site could be better

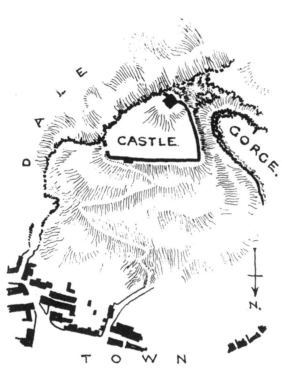

7. Peak Castle, Derbyshire.

Plan of the Site.

protected by nature.   The side next the gorge is absolutely inaccessible.   The side next the dale offers interesting hazards to good climbers.   The remaining side is a grass slope steeper than most modern roofs, and traversed by a zigzag path up which the breathless visitor toils painfully.   The town lies at the foot of the slope ; the castle, of no great extent, is placed at its summit. The keep is built in the extreme angle, where the gorge desists from finally biting its way through the side of the dale and leaves a narrow rugged strip of rock to connect the almost detached triangle from its parent hillside. A stone flung from one side of the keep would fall sheer down the gorge; flung from the opposite side would drop some 40 or 50 ft. on to the steep slope of the dale, and thence descend with huge and rapid bounds to the bottom.

The summit of the triangle was enclosed by a wall running from the gorge to the dale, thus forming a good-sized courtyard. It was of course on the slope, and to make it rather more level, the lower part was raised, partly it would seem on vaulted chambers, partly by filling up earth against the wall. These chambers have never been explored, but workmen who have repaired the wall bear testimony to their existence, and if the description they give of some of the articles found in them has been rightly interpreted, it would seem that the Romans had made use of them. This is still a matter for conjecture, and so is the exact arrangement of such buildings as were adjacent to the wall.

There were apparently two entrances to the court-yard. The chief of these was adjacent to the dale, and from the remains of the arch stones would appear to have been some 5 or 6 ft. wide. Here is said to have been the porter's rooms, and if this were the main entrance, custom would place the porter there. At the other end of the wall, against the gorge, are the remains of what has been called the sally-port; but the work has been so much defaced as to render its purpose obscure. Between these two features there is a rectangular buttressed projection which may have contained rooms, while overlooking the gorge is a recess in the wall which seems to have been a window. It is said—but

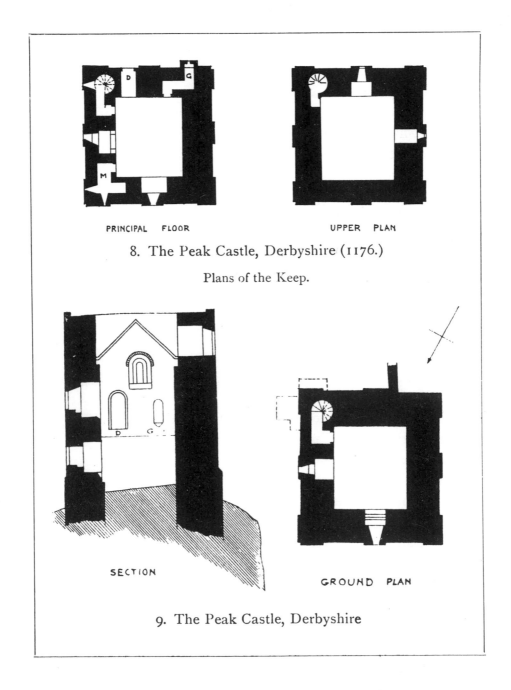

PRINCIPAL FLOOR   UPPER PLAN

8. The Peak Castle, Derbyshire (1176.)

Plans of the Keep.

SECTION   GROUND PLAN

9. The Peak Castle, Derbyshire

the statement has not been properly verified—that there are remains of the foundations of a structure which carried a drawbridge across the narrow upper end of the gorge; and it is almost certain that an ancient track leads along the hill on the further side of the gorge in the direction of the castle. All these points are of interest, and are worthy of further investigation; but that part of the ruins which most readily repays a visit is the keep. This has been described as merely a prison or a watch-tower; but from the carefully selected position of the castle, from what is known of its history, from the fact that the little town of Castleton clusters at its foot, and from a comparison with other castles, it would seem that the tower is the small keep of a small castle, and was its most secure dwelling-place. References in the great Roll of the Pipe show that a considerable number of soldiers were accommodated here; it is also recorded that in 1157 Malcolm of Scotland made his personal submission to Henry II. here, and that that king was again here in 1163, when the castle must have had even more restricted accommodation.

The keep itself, which was built in 1176, is very similar in arrangement to the peel-towers of the Scottish border and to the towers which elsewhere formed the nucleus of many fortified houses. It probably represents the first step in domestic planning, and may be regarded as one of the earliest ancestors of the great houses of later centuries.

It consisted of two main floors (Figs. 8, 9); beneath the lower was perhaps a store-room, although this is not certain. The debris with which the lower part of the building is filled has not been investigated; excavation might determine whether there ever was a cellar, and also whether there was any internal communication

with a natural cave or passage which undoubtedly passes
through the rock beneath it, and from which a tortuous
and difficult descent can be made to the great Peak
Cavern which is approached along the gorge so frequently mentioned.   Above the upper chamber was the
roof, originally of steep pitch (see section, Fig. 9), but
which may have been raised and flattened so as at once
to form a third chamber and to give more convenience
for the purposes of watching and defence.

At its best, at any rate, the keep can only have
contained four rooms, and it is quite possible that it
only had two.   The upper and better of these was that
into which the entrance door opened (at D, Fig. 8), a
door some 6 or 8 ft. from the ground, and doubtless
approached by a wood ladder.   Near this door a circular
staircase of about 5 ft. in diameter led up to the roof
and down to the lower room (Fig. 9), which was dimly
lighted by two small windows, but otherwise was devoid
of any feature whatever.   The floors were of wood.
The upper room, about 22 by 19 ft. in size, was also
lighted by two small windows; in one wall was a
garde-robe (G) with a shoot corbelled out from the wall;
in another was a small mural chamber (M) occupying
one corner of the building and lighted by a very small
window on two of its sides.   So far, this keep is just
like many others, although on a small scale; but here
there is no sign of a fireplace or flue.   Some means of
warming the place, and, on occasion, of cooking, there
must have been; and the probability is that a fire was
contrived on the floor, and that the smoke was carried
away by a flue of wood and plaster.   It would not have
been beyond the ingenuity of the time to provide a
hearth to carry the fire.

The exterior of the keep has suffered so much that
hardly any detail is left, nearly all the facing stone

having disappeared. The most perfect side is that towards the gorge, difficult of access (Fig. 10). From

10. The Peak Castle, Derbyshire (1176).
South west Face.

it, however, we learn that the building consisted of a plain mass of ashlar work broken at the angles and the middle of each side by a shallow projecting pier. Each corner of the building has a small circular shaft with cap and base of the ordinary Norman type. The window openings must have been narrow, as was usually the case, and probably of very simple detail, matching that of the doorway and the shoot of the *garde-robe.* At the parapet level there were probably four turrets rising from the angle buttresses, but all traces of them have gone. Indeed all that can be gathered of the external appearance is that it was of the usual severe type and that the detail was of the simplest.

While castles and their keeps were still in full occupation, but towards the later years of their existence, there were built a number of fortified manor houses of stone. It is quite probable that these buildings embodied in permanent materials a type of plan that had long prevailed in a less durable form. The keep was contrived so as to be as economical of space as possible; the rooms were piled one on the top of the other. But where defensive precautions were not so imperative, and space was not so valuable, the rooms were placed alongside of each other on the ground. The manor house, therefore, followed a type of plan somewhat different from that of the keep, but in both cases the hall was the principal apartment; it was the sleeping, eating, and living room of the household. As years went by the keep type of plan fell into disuse; its singular lack of comfort may easily account for this. The manor house type, on the contrary, survived, and it is this type which has been developed, through century after century, into the house of modern times. It is, however, curious to find a few late survivals of the keep, some of them built long after the necessity for castles had disappeared; others, owing to their geographical position, being the natural expression of the wants of the district. Among the former is Tattershall Castle in Lincolnshire, built by Lord Treasurer Cromwell in the fifteenth century, the same who built the great manor house of South Wingfield in Derbyshire. Both of these houses will be more fully mentioned in their chronological order. Among the latter are many of the peel-towers of Northumberland, which continued to be built with the ancient restricted arrangements until the accession of James I. Cocklaw Tower, near Hexham, is a fairly late example (Figs. 11, 12); it was built in the sixteenth century and contained hardly more accommodation than the Peak Castle. At the ground level was a cellar entered from the outside by a doorway protected by machicolations. Above the cellar was the hall, entered by an external door several feet above the ground, and above this was another room of the same size. Each of these rooms had a fireplace, and a few small windows,

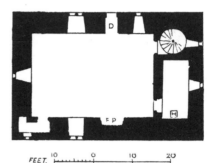

11. Cocklaw Tower, Northumberland (16th cent.).

Plan of Principal Floor.

D, Door, several feet above the level of the ground; H, Hole in floor; F P, Fireplace.

unglazed. A small chamber also led from each of them; that on the principal floor retains traces of painted decoration. In its floor is a square hole which afforded the only access to a blind chamber or vault beneath, which may have been a dungeon or may have been merely a *garde-robe* pit. A circular staircase led from the cellar to the upper floors and thence to the battlements. The fact that so small and uncomfortable a house was built at a time when further south there were already large and commodious mansions, is an eloquent commentary on the disturbed state of the Border.   This is further illustrated by the fact that almost immediately after the two kingdoms were united under one sovereign, many of the old peels were enlarged by the addition of a Jacobean wing of considerably greater capacity than

12. Cocklaw Tower, Northumberland (16th cent.).

the original house. Chipchase Castle is one of the most striking instances, as the new work took the form of a fair-sized manor house to which the peel became a mere antiquated adjunct. Other instances, some of rather later date, are to be seen at Belsay Castle. Halton Castle, and Bitchfield Tower.

Another notable example of the survival of the keep is that at Warkworth Castle in the same county (Fig. 45, p. 82). This is of peculiar interest inasmuch as it was built about the year 1440, and exhibits a great amount of skill in packing into a small compass the various rooms which, by that period, had become necessary to the comfort of the more wealthy. But in spite of the ingenious planning, this keep was deserted within thirty years of its erection in favour of a new hall built on the ground floor with contiguous kitchens in the usual fashion. These places are mentioned here before taking leave of the keep, to show how its influence survived long after it had been generally abandoned.

CHAPTER III.

The Fortified Manor House of the Thirteenth Century—The Dominance of the Hall.

ALTHOUGH the first germ of the house of to-day is to be found in the Norman keep, its more direct ancestor was the fortified manor house. The chief room here, as in the keep, was the hall; indeed it was of greater relative importance in the manor house than in the castle. In the latter it had rooms of equal size above and below it, rooms which must have helped to lessen the pressure on its space. In the former it was not so much the heart of the house as the house itself. It was often the only considerable room in the building, supplemented by a kitchen and a "chamber" or two. So overmastering was its importance that the house was called "the hall," a designation which, to this day, is applied to the principal house in a parish. There were, however, supplementary rooms, some for the master, and some for the servants; in the earlier examples, indeed, the plural is hardly admissible; there was one for the master, called the "solar," and there was a kitchen, or a kitchen department, which was the headquarters of the servants. The hall lay between the two; at one end was the kitchen with whatever it had of pantry and buttery; at the other was the solar, a small room for the private occupation of the lord—a room generally upstairs, and over a cellar or store place. Other rooms there were none. The hall was the house; everybody lived there when indoors, everybody ate there, everybody slept there.

> Knight, and page, and household squire,
> Loitered through the lofty hall,
> Or crowded round the ample fire.

The household stores, if put away anywhere, went to the cellar; the food was cooked in the kitchen, there was a pantry where it was kept when not in the kitchen, there was a buttery where the drink was served: the lord, when he desired privacy, sought his solar. The rest of the household presumably never had privacy even if they desired it. It was an elementary state of things, and the story of domestic architecture is made up of the efforts to obtain greater privacy and more comfort. It was a long and gradual development. The hall remained for centuries the centre and kernel of the house; but at one end of it the solar gradually swelled into suites of apartments for the family; at the other, the kitchen grew into the servants' wing, with scullery, larders, pantry, and many other subdivisions. When we remember this primitive type of plan and then look at the plan of an Elizabethan manor house (usually quite simple in its arrangements), it becomes less difficult to imagine the stages through which it must have passed since the time of the hall, solar, and kitchen; and it is easy, on the other hand, to see how the simple Elizabethan plan grew into the complicated arrangements necessary for our comfort to-day.

The hall, then, being pre-eminently the principal room, requires our first attention. It was necessarily of large size, and it was lofty. In the majority of instances it was of one storey with an open timber roof, and consequently it completely separated from each other the subsidiary rooms built at either end of it. This is observable down to Elizabethan days, when the family apartments and the servants' quarters had each grown into a considerable wing of at least two storeys in height. Each wing had to have its own staircases, and on the upper floor the hall interposed an impassable barrier between the two ends of the house.

The hall was planned so that the entrance was at the servants' end, where most of the traffic was. The bulk of the floor space was thus left clear for the tables, and for the purposes of daily life. The lord and his family sat at the "high table" at the upper end, farthest away from the draughty entrance. There was at this end a raised platform some 6 inches high, called the daïs, and it was on the daïs that the high table was placed. Judging from the floor levels of the earliest houses, there would not seem to have been a daïs, unless it were a movable platform. Through the wall at the upper end a doorway led to the family room or rooms. The two long sides of the hall were usually free from any buildings, and were occupied by the windows. At Minster Lovel in Oxfordshire, however—a splendid house of the Lovels, now in hopeless ruin—the lofty hall was flanked on one side with a building of two storeys. The windows on the opposite side were large and long, set fairly high up in the thick wall, of fine Perpendicular design, and finished at the top with the usual simple tracery. Those on the side flanked by the two-storey building were so much curtailed by it as to retain nothing below the tracery.

The entrance was generally cut off from the rest of the hall by a screen (at any rate in later years). The screen did not extend the full height of the hall, but stopped short some 10 or 12 ft. high, and was connected to the end wall by a floor, which thus at once served as a ceiling to the entrance passage, and formed a gallery, usually called the minstrels' gallery, though indeed it may well be doubted whether in many of the smaller houses it was put to regular use, inasmuch as there was no convenient means of access. The fire was frequently, though not by any means always, placed on a hearth in the middle of the floor, yet not exactly the middle, but rather towards the end where the family sat. There are plenty of instances where the hall was warmed by a fireplace even in fairly early times. There are also instances as late as the sixteenth century of hearths being constructed on the floor. At Deene Hall in Northamptonshire, built in the time of Edward VI., there was no fireplace in the hall until the father of the late Lord Cardigan (of Balaclava fame) caused one to be made. The roof shows by the absence of cross-braces in one of its bays where the louvre for the escape of smoke used to stand.

These general dispositions were, of course, subject to variations in particular instances, but the main idea of entering the hall at its lower end, of the kitchens being at this end and the solar or family rooms at the other, is so universal as to furnish a clue to the unravelling of the mysteries of many a complicated ruin.

The finest example in England of an early hall is to be found at Oakham Castle in Rutland. It is of such a large size, 65 ft. long by 43 ft. wide, that it serves for the Law Courts of the county, the Assizes, Quarter Sessions, and County Court being all held within its four walls. The fittings necessary for these purposes rather obscure its original appearance, which was as spacious as a good-sized parish church, and very much of the same character. It is divided into what may be termed nave and aisles separated by fine bold arcades (Fig. 13).

This disposition is extremely interesting, as it at once raises the question of the resemblance between ecclesiastical and domestic architecture, and takes us immediately to the root of the matter, namely, that architecture is essentially a noble form of construction, embellished suitably to its purpose.   It follows, therefore, that church and house architecture are only likely to differ in so far as their purposes differ.   Here at Oakham was a space to be covered of much the same area as a church, and it was covered in the same way.   The

13. Oakham Castle.
Interior of the Hall.

means at the disposal of the builders forbade very wide spans, therefore they divided the width of the building by two walls carried on a series of arches.   The middle space (or nave) was of no greater width than could be covered by a timber roof resting on the arcaded walls. The two outer spaces (or aisles) were covered by narrower roofs leaning against the walls of the nave.

This simple solution of a constructional problem was applied equally to churches or houses, but it so happens that there were many churches of a width demanding such a treatment and but few houses. The churches have survived, while the houses have mostly disappeared ; and consequently the disposition which is in reality constructional, has become associated with church architecture. So too with various features, such as doors and windows. These were treated, broadly speaking, in the same way whether in churches or houses, but in the former they were, as a rule, more elaborately embellished. Their general forms were the same ; that is to say, when arches were round in churches they were round in houses ; when pointed in the one they were pointed in the other. When mullions, tracery, and cusping became the fashion in churches, they became also, though in less degree, the fashion in houses. This, however, is to be observed that, as a rule, more elaboration and more fancy were bestowed upon ecclesiastical work than upon domestic. So far as windows are concerned the practical necessity of having some means of opening and closing those in houses led to the dividing of them into manageable sizes by means of horizontal cross-bars or transomes, which are much more frequent in houses than in churches.

This similarity of treatment between the two classes of buildings, although only what might be expected on reflection, has led to much confusion in the popular mind, and has resulted in many an old hall being looked upon as a chapel.

But to return to Oakham Castle. Strictly speaking it was not a castle, but merely a strongly defended manor house. It lies in a large enclosure surrounded by the ruins of a wall. The wall shows no signs of having been guarded by the towers customary in a castle, but is built on the summit of an embankment, which may be the remains of an extremely ancient stronghold. The height and steepness of the bank, increased by the height of the wall, although the latter was ill-constructed, must have rendered attack difficult. The enclosure was entered through a gate-house, which has entirely disappeared and only lives in a record of the fourteenth century. This record is an Inquisition of the year 1340, and is interesting as

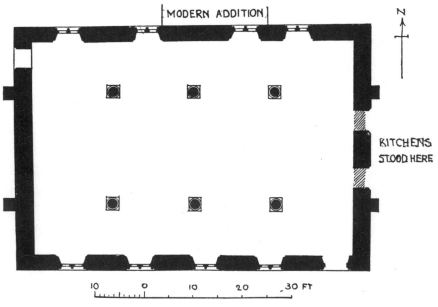

14. Oakham Castle, Rutland (*cir.* 1180).
The Hall.

enumerating the accommodation of the place at the time. It says that the castle was well walled, and contained one hall, four chambers, and one kitchen ; there were also two stables, one grange for hay, one house for prisoners, one chamber for the porter, and one draw-bridge with iron chains (this indicates the gatehouse). There was also a free chapel within the castle. Such was the accommodation of an important house in the fourteenth century.

The hall is the only building left, and it is clear from its architectural features that the four chambers and the kitchen could only have been of one storey in height, at any rate so far as they were contiguous to the building. The overpowering importance of the hall is thus further

15. Oakham Castle, Rutland (*cir.* 1180).

The Hall.

The door was originally at the right-hand end of the front. The original window in the gable is shown as blocked up; that immediately above the doors is of late date.

established. Its plan is of the usual type (Fig. 14). The entrance door was at the end of one of its sides, although many years ago it was removed, for greater convenience in relation to modern uses, to its present position in the middle.

In the end adjacent to the entrance were two doors

(there are also indications of a third at the end of the
north aisle) which led to the kitchen, the pantry, and
buttery. At the upper end was a door which led to the
solar and subsequently, no doubt, to the four chambers,
mentioned in the Inquisition, which replaced it. At the
time when the hall was built, about 1180, the probability
is that there were not so many as four chambers, but
merely the solar. There is no fireplace, so the fire must
have been on a central hearth, with a louvre over it in
the roof; but the present roof having been rebuilt
affords no evidence on this point. The lighting was
from small windows in the side walls, supplemented by
a larger one in the gable over the doors to the kitchen
(Fig. 15). The side walls are necessarily not very
lofty, and the light from the small windows had a long
way to travel, consequently the place must have been
but ill-lighted although far more cheerful than contemporary keeps. The lighting was wholly inadequate
for modern purposes, and has therefore been increased
by means of dormers.

The style of the work is such as marks the buildings
of the later years of the twelfth century. The four
arches of the arcades are semicircular and of about
15 ft. span; they rest on massive round pillars (Fig. 13),
and where they spring from the end walls they rest on
corbels of unusual and quaint design. The entrance
door is round-headed and of two orders, the outer being
carried on a shaft and cap. The windows are of two
lights, with pointed heads, the mouldings carried on
shafts externally; the tympanum is filled in solid, thus
making the actual light square-headed. Internally each
window is set in a deep recess under a round-headed
arch carried down to the floor, thus differing from
church windows which usually have a sill the full thickness of the wall. The angles of the windows inside and

out, as well as the outer angles of the doorway, are ornamented with the dog-tooth. The illustrations make this short description plainer than many words, and they show how in general treatment the door and windows closely resemble contemporary work in churches.

There are no indications of a screen at the entrance end, nor of a daïs at the upper, inasmuch as the ornament of the window recesses goes down to the floor in all cases, whereas had there been a permanent daïs, it would have stopped short to accommodate it.

The pillars of the arcade have vigorously carved caps admirably designed (Fig. 16), and they support, between the springing of the arches, quaint figures of musicians. Two of the heads which support a corbel on the wall near the entrance are supposed to represent Henry II. and his queen.

16. Oakham Castle.

Pier cap.

The whole of the work is excellent in design and execution, and the hall, both in its arrangement and its building, is the most valuable example left of its period.

The hall at Oakham is typical, as to its main features, of all others down to the end of the sixteenth century. That is to say, the hall was the principal room; it was entered through the screens; at the lower end were the kitchens, at the upper the family rooms. It was nearly always a lofty apartment of one storey with an open timber roof. The principal changes that took

C

place in the room itself were the elimination of the pillars and the contriving of a roof to cover it in one span from wall to wall ; the provision of larger windows, and especially of a bay window at the daïs end ; the addition of a porch to protect the front entrance from the weather.   The other changes which affected it were those which took place in the rooms at either end ; the

17. Cothele House, Cornwall (time of Henry VII.).

The Great Hall.

growth of the solar into a suite of rooms, and the provision of separate sleeping accommodation for the servants. By the end of the sixteenth century these changes had very materially affected the size and plan of the house, and they ultimately led to the extinction of the hall as a living room ; but this development will be further considered in a later chapter.

An illustration of a late hall (of the time of Henry VII.) is given in Fig. 17, from Cothele House in Cornwall. It shows the large window, the fireplace, and the start of the open roof. The daïs has disappeared, as it has in most old houses, but the door leading to the family rooms is visible in the corner. It gives a good idea of the appearance of a mediæval hall.

All the changes which took place in the treatment of dwellings tended towards the increase of comfort. The growth, it is true, was slow, and if a modern critic were compelled to dwell in them, the difference to him between a house of the twelfth century and one of the thirteenth would hardly be perceptible; both would be intolerable. But gradually the number of rooms increased both at the upper and lower ends of the hall. The keep still survived in a modified form, and often formed the nucleus round which the rest of the house grew. At Stokesay in Shropshire, which dates from about 1240, or sixty years later than Oakham, there is still a keep, but it is almost detached from the actual house, and may have served as the final stronghold to which the inhabitants could retreat in times of stress. At Longthorpe in Northamptonshire, some two miles to the west of Peterborough, there is a very interesting though small example of a keep or peel-tower attached to the house, and forming an integral part of it. The house was built in the latter part of the thirteenth century, and has undergone many alterations; but the tower remains in good preservation, as also does a contemporary gable adjacent to it, the only remnant of the original house.

The most usual method of protecting these manor houses was to surround them with a moat, across which a drawbridge led to a strongly defended gateway. Bodiam Castle in Sussex, on the borders of Kent

(Fig. 18), is an excellent example of a moated structure. It was built in 1386 as a place of defence, rather than as a dwelling-house.   In hilly districts moats were impossible, and in such cases advantage was taken of a precipitous piece of ground which might furnish natural protection on as many sides as possible.   Aydon Castle in Northumberland is a striking instance of the

18. Bodiam Castle, Sussex (1386).

Showing the Moat.

latter kind of defence, being situated on the edge of a ravine.   Although inhabited, it still retains much of its original appearance, and many of its original features.

Stokesay (about 1240-1290) was defended by a moat, crossed no doubt by a drawbridge, and entered through a gatehouse.   The original fortified gatehouse, however, has been replaced by a picturesque half-timber structure of Elizabeth's time, and the drawbridge by a solid approach. The gateway led into a large courtyard, on the opposite side of which stood, and still stands, the house (see plan, Fig. 19). The chief apartment, as usual, is the hall, not so large as that at Oakham, but still of fair size, 52 by 31 ft., that is to say large enough to contain, with plenty of space to spare, two complete

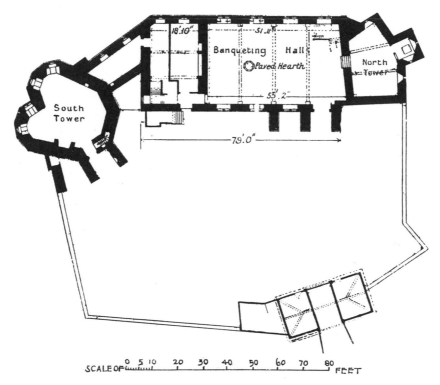

19. Stokesay Castle, Shropshire (*cir.* 1240-90).

Ground Plan.

houses such as now form the streets of a growing town. It is covered with a simply designed open timber roof (see section, Fig. 20), the principal rafters of which rest on plain built-out corbels. There were no buttresses to counteract its thrust, until it was found necessary to build some on the courtyard side. Unlike Oakham, the

hall at Stokesay has rooms attached to it at each end.
At the lower end they are of three storeys, at the upper
of two. Applying the usual rule the three-storeyed
part (marked on the plan "North Tower") ought to
have been for the servants' or retainers' use; and it
is possible that in early days it was. The lowest
storey was doubtless a cellar, the upper ones, however,
are furnished with large fireplaces, which point to their
occupation by a superior class of persons. In later years
the topmost room was en-
larged and made more
cheerful by adding some
overhanging half - timber
work in which plenty of
windows were introduced
(Fig. 21). The kitchen
must have stood at this
end, but there are no
remains of it left. There
was at one time a return
wing running east from
the north tower; it was
built of wood, and con-
tained kitchens, probably
of a date subsequent to
the hall. These rooms at the lower end were approached by a wooden stair within the hall, a rather
unusual arrangement. From the upper end of the hall
access was obtained by an external flight of stone steps
to the solar, or lord's chamber, which had a large fireplace, and on either side of it a small window looking
into the hall, so that the lord—or more probably, considering the immutability of human nature, the lady—
could overlook that apartment after retiring from it.
The solar was embellished in later times with panelling

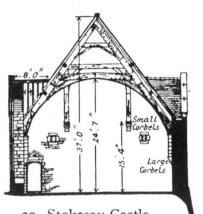

20. Stokesay Castle.

Section of Great Hall.

In the end wall are two
small windows opening
from the solar.

21. Stokesay Castle (General View).

The hall and adjoining rooms are to the right ; the south tower is in the centre ; the Elizabethan gatehouse to the left.

and a fine wood chimney-piece, and thus rendered a
very pleasant room. Beneath the solar was, as usual,
a cellar or store place on the ground floor, and beneath
that another cellar underground. Outside and beyond
the solar stands the massive south tower or keep of three
storeys, with one room on each floor. They have fireplaces, but the windows are small, and were never
glazed, but merely closed with shutters.

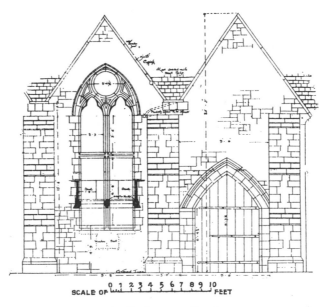

SCALE OF　0 1 2 3 4 5 6 7 8 9 10　FEET

22. Stokesay Castle.

Window and Doorway of the Hall.

It must be borne in mind that hitherto windows
had not been glazed. They were usually of small size
for purposes of security, and no doubt their smallness
was an advantage so far as the inlet of cold air was
concerned. But they rendered the rooms gloomy to the
last degree, and the unlucky people of the time must
often have had the choice of two evils, icy draughts, or
the darkness which followed the closing of the shutters.
No wonder the fireplaces were made large, yet even

with a blazing fire in the middle of the hall, none of its heat being lost up the chimney, the plight of the household must have resembled that of travellers round a camp fire who complain of being roasted on one side and frozen on the other.

In the hall at Stokesay, however, the windows are large, and the lights are of such ample width as to offer but little protection against attack. They are two lights wide and two lights high, the upper ones being pointed and cusped, and surmounted by a circular eye (Fig. 22). This eye and the upper lights were glazed, but the lower ones were merely closed with shutters. This amount of glazing is a decided advance in comfort, and so is the size of the windows, which must have rendered the hall quite a cheerful place, in striking contrast to the gloom of the tower, where the small windows provide a patch of

23. Stokesay Castle.

Window in South Tower—Showing shutter and stone seats.

light which only renders the general darkness more pronounced (Fig. 23).

The glazing of windows was carried out in a fitful way. Some windows in buildings as early as Stokesay were already glazed, others even so late as the end of the fifteenth century were not so treated. In the scanty remains of Abingdon Abbey the so-called Prior's Room has never had glass in its windows. This room is of the early Decorated period (c. 1300) and whether devoted to the prior or not, it was of sufficient importance to have a fine fireplace and plastered walls ornamented with coloured lines. The windows of the adjoining guest-house (if such were its purpose) have likewise never been glazed. These are of much later date—towards the end of the fifteenth century. They, too, lighted rooms of some importance, 30 ft. long, warmed by a large fire, handsomely roofed, and decorated in places with elaborate ornament.* Horn was occasionally used as a material for glazing prior to the general use of glass.

The improvement in domestic arrangements which is observable in the actual buildings at Stokesay is also noticeable in such contemporary accounts of building works as have been preserved. The Liberate Rolls of Henry III.'s time (1232-1269) contain many orders issued in respect of the king's houses which were scattered up and down the country in almost every southern county from Kent to Hereford, and northwards to Northamptonshire and Nottingham. They nearly all point towards making the houses more comfortable. Windows were to be glazed to prevent draughts ; porches were to be built to external doors ; passages of communication were to be made from one building to another ; roofs and walls were to be wainscoted ; windows were to be enlarged ; fireplaces were to be built ; *garde-robes* were to be made less offensive ; in some cases drainage was to be executed as a protection to health. Everything goes to show that Henry's aim was to make his houses more convenient and more comfortable. In addition to structural alterations there are many orders for decoration. Buildings were to be

---

* Remains of this are visible in the plastered spaces of one of the principals.

whitewashed inside and out; windows were to be filled with painted glass, either heraldic or setting forth some scriptural subject, notably the story of Dives and Lazarus; shutters were to be painted with the king's arms; and most frequently of all, rooms were to be painted green spangled with gold stars. It is quite clear that houses were gradually becoming not merely places of safety and of shelter from winter and rough weather, but places of pleasure and delight; not merely lairs but homes.

CHAPTER IV.

The Course of Mediæval Building in the Fourteenth Century.

THE king, of course, may be supposed to have had unlimited means at his disposal for the improvement of his houses, and to have been better able than less exalted personages to gratify his wishes ; but his subjects were also actuated by the same desires, and an examination of the large houses of the fourteenth century shows a considerable advance in the provision of rooms for special purposes, and indicates that the old restricted accommodation was no longer sufficient for the changing habits of the time. This expansion of the house was general, and was not confined to any particular district. To mention a few instances, there are in the North Alnwick Castle, built by the Percys about 1340, of which all but the external walls has been modernised ; and Raby Castle, the home of the Nevills, Earls of Westmorland, built about 1378, also largely modernised. In the Midlands are Kenilworth Castle, almost rebuilt by John of Gaunt in the closing years of the fourteenth century ; Warwick Castle, also almost entirely rebuilt by Thomas Beauchamp, Earl of Warwick, a few years earlier ; Broughton Castle in Oxfordshire, built by the De Broughtons about the beginning of the fourteenth century ; Drayton House in Northamptonshire, by Simon de Drayton in 1328 ; and Haddon Hall in Derbyshire, where the greater part of the work is of this period. In the South is Penshurst Place for which a licence to crenellate was granted to John de Pulteney in 1341.

The smaller houses of this period do not, of course, show such extensive improvements as the large places just mentioned, nevertheless in them may be seen the same tendency towards greater civilisation. Even in the far North, where the disturbed state of the Border retarded the development of household comfort, we have the commodious house of Naworth in Cumberland, and the smaller house of Yanwath in Westmorland. In Yorkshire is Markenfield Hall; in Cheshire, Baguley, of which little besides its timber hall is left; in Northamptonshire the small but fine house at North-borough; in Berkshire is Sutton Courtney, so much altered, however, as to have lost its original character; while in Somerset is the very curious "Castle" of Nunney, where the rooms are placed over each other more after the fashion of the earlier keeps than of the long and low manor houses which were by this time the prevailing type.

In all these houses the hall was still the chief apartment, but it is supplemented by more subsidiary rooms than are to be found in earlier examples. The references in contemporary literature and documents are not numerous, but we have already seen that at Oakham in the Inquisition of 1340 the house consisted of a hall, four chambers, and a kitchen. If we turn to Chaucer, who lived during a large part of the fourteenth century, dying in 1400, we find in the few incidental references to domestic arrangements which occur that the hall was by far the most important room, although it had "chambers" and a "bower" to supplement it.

It is perhaps from the "Cook's Tale of Gamelyn" that the best idea of a house may be gained, with its gate-house, courtyard, and turreted hall. He tells us how his muscular hero Gamelyn, the prototype of Shake-speare's Orlando, came with his friends to his ancestral home, held by his false brother, and how the gate was shut and locked against them by the porter, who resolutely refused them admission to the courtyard. Gamelyn, however, smote the wicket with his foot, broke the pin and effected an entrance. The porter he chased across the yard, broke his neck and threw him into a well. He and his friends then made merry with the brother's meat and wine, while the latter hid himself in a "little turret," for which we owe him our thanks, as showing that such features had a use. Meanwhile the gate had been flung open to admit all who cared to go in "or ride," a touch which brings home to us the fact that hardly any of these gatehouses were wide enough to admit wheeled vehicles, which of course were somewhat rare in those days; the entrances were contrived only for foot passengers and horsemen. Presently the fortunes of the day changed, Gamelyn was overpowered and bound to a post in the hall, and the false brother emerged from the "selleer" (solar) to taunt him. For two days and nights Gamelyn stood bound without meat or drink, but then, thinking he had fasted too long, he besought Adam the "spencer" to free him. Adam hesitated to let him go out of "this bour," but ultimately consented, and took him into the "spence" and gave him supper. The spence was the pantry, and the spencer the presiding genius of that place. It would be beside the mark to enter into the details of Gamelyn's further adventures, suffice it to say that by Adam's advice he let himself appear to be still bound to the post; the hall presently filled with his brother's guests who cast their eyes on the captive as they came in "at hall door." At a preconcerted signal, Gamelyn and Adam possessed themselves of some stout cudgels which the good spencer had provided, and between them they cudgelled the whole company, taking especial delight in dealing with the " men of holy Church."

This glimpse into a fourteenth-century mansion is the longest which Chaucer vouchsafes ; we read else-where of " halls, chambers, kitchens, and bowers," and the " chamber " is occasionally mentioned as the alterna-tive room to the hall so far as the owner and his wife are concerned. The difference between a " bower " and a " chamber " does not emerge very clearly. Adam, as we have seen, speaks of the hall as " this bour," but as a rule the term is applied to a room in order to dis-tinguish it from that apartment. It seems quite clear that to Chaucer the hall was the chief room, almost synonymous with the house, the other rooms he mentions being the merest accessories.

The most complete and most interesting house of this period is the well-known Haddon Hall in Derby-shire. It consists of two courts (Fig. 24), the hall being placed in the wing which divides them. It is thus protected on both of its long sides and is thereby enabled to have larger windows than if it had been on an outside wall. The exterior walls of the earlier parts of Haddon have comparatively few windows in them, and these of small size ; and as the kitchen is one of the rooms so lighted it is dark, in spite of a larger window inserted in the sixteenth century, to a degree which horrifies house-wives of the present day. Haddon being built on the slope of a hill could not be protected by a moat, hence it was more than ever necessary to be careful about external apertures. Some parts of Haddon are of the twelfth century, including much of the west wall, portions of the chapel (at the south-west corner), and the lower parts of the south and east walls and of the Peverel or Eagle tower ; the licence granted to Richard de Vernon to fortify his house of Haddon with a wall 12 ft. high

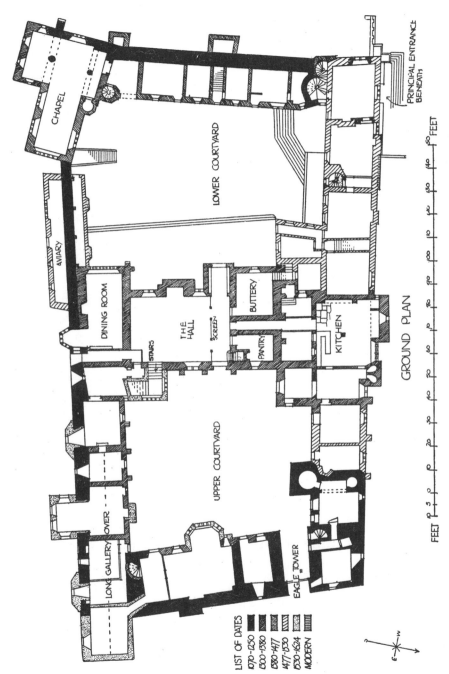

24. Plan of Haddon Hall, Derbyshire.

without crenellations is still preserved. This licence was granted by John, Earl of Morteigne, who, in 1199, became King John. The extent of this early work shows that already in the twelfth century there was a large house here, its area being little less than at the present day. But during the fourteenth century it was practically rebuilt on the lines which now remain, inasmuch as work of this period is to be found over the whole building. The extent of the house, and particularly the multiplicity of rooms, go to show how vastly the desire for comfort had increased by this time. Much other work was done in later years ; the chapel was either enlarged or altered, and a range of rooms was added or rebuilt in the fifteenth century. In the early part of the sixteenth many of the rooms were embellished and modernised by Sir George Vernon, "the King of the Peak" ; and yet later his daughter Dorothy and her husband Sir John Manners built the beautiful long gallery on the top of earlier rooms and laid out the garden with its picturesque terraces and noble flight of steps.

It is of great interest to see here the work of various hands, and to realise how, generation after generation, the owners did what they could to bring their ancient home up to the prevailing standard of comfort and beauty. But the particular point which is of interest now is that although much of the existing work is of later date, yet it is clear that in the fourteenth century Haddon was of almost the same extent as we see it to-day. Civilisation had taken many strides since its little neighbour, the Peak Castle, had been built.

It is curious to observe on a plan of the house how much thicker the external walls are than the internal, and how few windows look outwards ; they nearly all look into the courts, and of those that look out over the country most are of later date. The plan also shows very clearly how the disposition of the hall follows the orthodox lines. It is entered through a porch at the end of one of its sides; the porch leads into the "screens"; on the right is the hall entered through a panelled wood screen with two openings. On the left are three doorways—one to the buttery, one to the kitchen passage, and the third to the pantry. At the end of the screens is a door leading into the upper court. The kitchen department is large, rambling, and ill-lighted, but when the house was in full occupation an enormous amount of work had to be done here, and doubtless the fire itself sufficiently supplemented the scanty daylight.

At the upper end of the hall is a range of rooms of two storeys, devoted to the use of the family; and doubtless in the fourteenth century it was already of two storeys, although apparently it only extended at that period from the front or west side of the hall as far eastwards as to overlap the east side of the upper court. It is difficult to disentangle these rooms from the additions and alterations of later years, for in the early part of the sixteenth century the rooms immediately contiguous to the south end of the hall were improved, and a new range was built on the top of the curtain wall, which ran from the hall wing westwards to the chapel. Again, towards the close of the same century, the long gallery was built over the ground floor rooms forming the south side of the upper court, and apparently this wing was prolonged in order to give that extreme length to the gallery which was so characteristic of Elizabeth's time. This prolongation carried the south front beyond the line of the east front, an arrangement very unlikely to have been adopted while the house was still fortified.

Another curious and instructive feature is the gallery or gangway which is carried along the east side of the hall. This is not an original gallery, but was erected in order to connect the south rooms with those on the north, which previously had been completely severed from each other by the lofty hall.

Haddon Hall, therefore, taken as a fourteenth-century dwelling, shows that protection from casual attack was still essential, but that there was a great amount of separate accommodation for the members of the household. The rooms, however, were arranged without much regard to convenience. They were placed in long and somewhat straggling ranges of single apartments leading one into the other. Privacy was much more studied than it had been in the preceding centuries, but it was provided to a degree that falls far short of modern requirements.

The fact that the only entrance through which a wheeled vehicle could enter the place was a secondary archway up the hill beneath the Eagle Tower, brings home to us again the fact that the usual means of locomotion was at that time either on foot or on horseback.

The view (Fig. 25) is taken in the lower courtyard, looking towards the great hall. The entrance door is placed in a projecting porch, over which a low tower is carried up. The staircase to the upper part of the tower is in an octagonal turret, which rises in picturesque fashion sufficiently high above the roof to give access to the leads. To the right of the porch is the great chimney-stack of the hall, now deprived of its original tall shaft. Beyond the chimney is one of the fourteenth-century windows of the hall with simple but characteristic tracery. Then comes the projecting end of the dining-room with its early sixteenth-century window of many lights in width, but only one in height; above this is a later window, not so wide, but divided into three lights as to its height. The return wing on the right contains the rooms, built early in the sixteenth century over the

25. Haddon Hall, Derbyshire (View in the Lower Courtyard).

original wall of the twelfth century. The interest of
the composition is increased by the absence of large
windows on the ground floor of this wing, where, as the
plan indicates, there was no need to have them.

Another great house, dating largely from late in the
fourteenth century, is Kenilworth Castle, which, though
primarily a place of strength, has much that is interesting purely as domestic architecture. It has been held
by kings and great nobles ; some of the most celebrated
names in English history are linked with its story ; it
has withstood sieges, when its walls enclosed despairing
and disease-stricken men ; it has witnessed the most
gorgeous pageants of a gorgeous age. Reality and
romance have vied to make it famous. It is worthy of
far more careful study than can be bestowed upon it
here, where it can only be briefly used to throw its light
on the progress of domestic architecture through some
four centuries. As a fortified place of dwelling it goes
back to Saxon times ; as a stone house it was occupied
between four and five hundred years ; it has been a
ruin for nearly three hundred. In extent the site is
very considerable, embracing some eight or nine acres
of fortified enclosure (Fig. 26), but the walls, the towers,
and the gateways which made its defences ; the ditches,
the moat, and the pool or lake which further secured it,
do not fall within the range of the present inquiry ; it is
only the inner or upper ward which need detain us. The
earliest of the buildings which form this ward is the great
keep, situated at the north-east corner, the home of the
family in Norman times. In its main characteristics it
resembled the other large keeps which have been already
described (Chapter II.), and its date may be placed at the
end of the third quarter of the twelfth century. There
must have been other contemporary buildings somewhere
in the vast enclosure, mostly of wood, but some also of

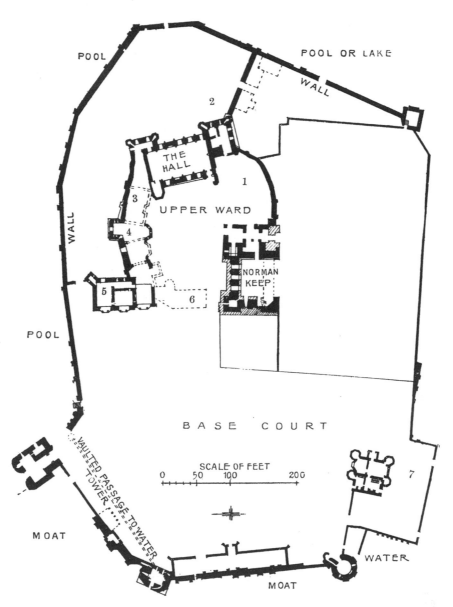

26. Kenilworth Castle, Warwickshire.

Ground Plan.

1. Site of Kitchens.   4. Garde-robe Tower.
2. The Strong Tower.   5. Leicester's Buildings.
3. The White Hall.   6. Henry VIII.'s Lodgings.
7. Elizabethan Gate-house.

stone: they have, however, all disappeared, and it is only from scattered fragments of early work that their character can be surmised. Doubtless during the next two centuries the descendants of the builders, the Clintons, or those who displaced them—the king, Simon de Montfort, Edmund, Earl of Lancaster, son of Henry III., Roger Mortimer, and the rest—added to the meagre and comfortless accommodation of their predecessors. Indeed it is on record that large sums were expended on buildings and repairs during the reigns of John and Henry III. But anything they may have built must have been swept away in the great rebuilding undertaken by John of Gaunt towards the end of the fourteenth century, about 1392; and it is not improbable from the irregular shape of the plan that his new buildings followed the main lines of those they superseded. By far the greater part of the upper ward is of this date. Starting from the west end of the keep, the kitchens on the north (now almost entirely gone), the great hall on the west, the white hall and other chambers on the south, are all John of Gaunt's work. Where he left off, Dudley, Earl of Leicester, began, nearly two hundred years later; and although Leicester's buildings are fairly large in themselves, they are small in comparison with those of "time-honoured Lancaster."

The range of chambers built by John of Gaunt shows how enormously domestic requirements had increased since the days when the restricted accommodation of a keep had sufficed for the housing of the lord and his family; or those when the subsidiary rooms attached to so fine a hall as that at Oakham were merely four "chambers" and a kitchen. The great hall, 90 ft. long by 45 ft. wide, occupied nearly the whole of the west front. It stood on a vaulted undercroft (see section, Fig. 27), and was entered at the north end of its east

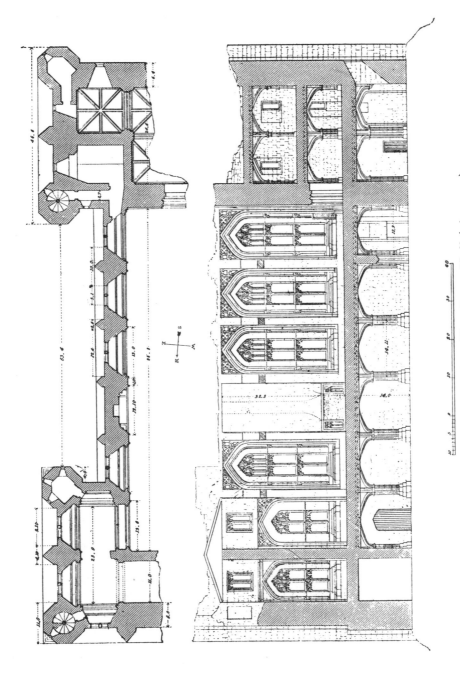

27. Kenilworth Castle.   The Great Hall (*cir.* 1392).

The upper figure shows the plan of one side : the lower is the longitudinal section through the hall and undercroft.

side up a flight of steps, which eventually led into the
" screens." To the right or north of the entrance were
the buttery, the kitchen, and other servants' quarters.

28. Kenilworth Castle.
A Window of the Great Hall.

Beyond them, and projecting on the west front, was a
tower called the Strong Tower, used as a place of de-
tention for persons of consequence, some of whom have

here, as others in the Tower of London, left melancholy mementoes of weary hours in the shape of their coats-of-arms scratched upon the walls.

The hall itself was a noble apartment, admirably built in the best period of the Perpendicular style, lighted by large and lofty windows (Figs. 27, 28), and covered with an open timbered roof, which has long since disappeared. It must have been one of the finest halls of its time. At the upper or daïs end there is, on the east side, an octagonal bay window, with a fireplace in the south-west corner; while on the west is a tower, used on this floor as a buffet, and giving access by a passage to the range of rooms on the south front which were rooms of state and family apartments. About midway along their south front stood a large *garde-robe* tower. The two towers which project from the west front and balance each other at either end of the hall are a foretaste of the symmetry which was, in later years, to play so important a part in the disposition of great houses. The general arrangement of the hall, with the kitchens at one end and the family rooms at the other, conforms to the usual type so frequently mentioned, which may also be seen very clearly at Haddon. The bay window at the daïs end is an early example of an arrangement which afterwards became universal. The hall fire was not placed on the floor in the middle of that apartment, but in two fireplaces, one in either side wall about half way between the screen and the daïs.

The planning is, as usual, wasteful; the same accommodation might have been obtained with far less outlay and much more convenience, and a study of Elizabethan plans shows how far more surely and much more cheaply the designer of that day obtained his effects than did his predecessor of the fourteenth century.

There can be no doubt that the Elizabethan designer

aimed at effect as well as at convenience of arrangement. But it is doubtful how far the designer of the fourteenth century had both these objects in view. No doubt he sought for effect in each building ; that is to say, he strove to produce a noble hall, an impressive tower, a pleasant range of minor buildings. But his general arrangements were mostly haphazard ; he built as circumstances dictated, either following the lines of previous buildings, or hurriedly placing his new rooms where at first sight they seemed to be wanted, without much caring whether they came awkwardly or not.

29. Kenilworth Castle—View from the North-west.
(The keep is on the left ; the great hall on the right.)

He probably had an eye for the picturesque, for it is doubtful whether all the towers and turrets which broke his skyline were built for necessity. Here at Kenilworth he displayed, as already remarked, some feeling for symmetry on the west front. When Leicester came to build his addition on the east, towards the end of the sixteenth century, there can be little doubt that considerations of symmetry dictated the form of the buildings, for instead of adopting the long and low fashion then so much in vogue, he piled his rooms up in order to balance the lofty mass of the ancient keep. This is very apparent on a view made in 1620,* where these two large blocks are joined by a low range of buildings called " Henry VIII.'s Lodgings," which have since then been entirely destroyed.

The view (Fig. 29) shows the Norman keep on the left, and the range containing the fourteenth-century hall on the right. The difference of treatment between the two periods is plainly visible. The keep is massive and stern with but few windows; the hall is lighter and more graceful, partly owing to its lofty windows, and partly to the vertical lines of its turrets and projections.

So far the hall has been the principal room that has claimed attention, although at Haddon and Kenilworth we find it supplemented by other chambers for the use of the family and servants. The latter, however, had not yet assumed any special architectural importance; in this respect the most notable building, next to the hall, appears to have been the kitchen.

In early times the kitchen, as already said, was detached from the house, and often of so temporary a nature that no examples have survived; but in later years it became one of the most important and substantially built parts of the house. It was still frequently a detached or outlying building of one lofty storey, connected with the house, as at Raby Castle in Durham, the Abbot's kitchen in Durham itself (1368), the Abbot's kitchen at Glastonbury (c. 1400), that at Stanton Harcourt in Oxfordshire (c. 1470), and that at Burghley House, Northamptonshire (c. 1550). But more often it was incorporated with the house itself, and had rooms

---

* See an engraving made after a drawing of 1716 from the original painting in fresco at Newnham Padox, published by Henry Merridew, Coventry.

over it as at Haddon Hall (fourteenth century), and South Wingfield (1435-40).

At Glastonbury the kitchen is square, each corner being occupied by a fireplace the arch over which carries a wall, converting the space above into an octagon (see plan, Fig. 30). The octagon is carried up to a height of some 20 ft., and is then vaulted on eight stone ribs up to a ventilating shaft (see section, Fig. 30). The height from the floor to the bottom of the ventilating shaft is 41 ft.; the kitchen itself is 33 ft. 10 in. square. The flues from the fireplaces were apparently carried up into chimney shafts, which stood on the

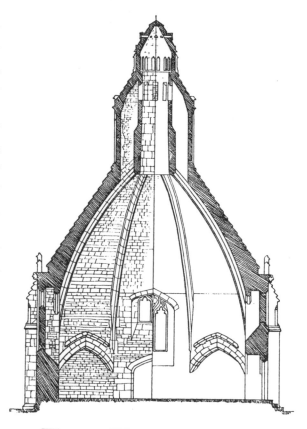

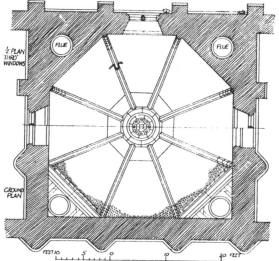

30. The Kitchen, Glastonbury Abbey.
Plan and Section.

31. The Kitchen, Glastonbury Abbey (*cir.* 1400).

triangular space between the square corners of the building and the octagonal roof, but the shafts have entirely disappeared (Fig. 31). The remains of the walls which connected this kitchen with the adjacent buildings are still visible.

The kitchen at Stanton Harcourt is not quite so elaborate. It is nearly square on plan, being 25 ft. 9 in. one way, by 25 ft. 6 in. the other—considerably smaller, therefore, than the Glastonbury example (see plan, Fig. 32). There seems to have been no special flue from the fireplace, which must have been on an open hearth, the smoke finding its way up to the roof, and thence through louvred openings. The height here is nearly as great as that at Glastonbury, being 39 ft. to the bottom of the roof. The roof is octagonal on plan, the four corners of the square building being gathered over on squinches. It is of wood covered with stone slates, and is carried on eight curved half principals which meet in the centre. The lower part of the roof is vertical, and is filled with windows and louvre boards for the escape of the smoke on alternate forces of the octagon (see section, Fig. 32). Above the vertical part, it slopes up to a great heraldic finial. The top of the stone walls is battlemented, the space between the parapet and the octagonal lantern forming a kind of parapet walk, access to which is obtained up a circular staircase placed in a square projecting turret at one corner (Fig. 33). There are the usual two ovens (one large and one small) in the thickness of the wall, and there is also a recess probably used as a cupboard. There is a door in each corner, three for access from other parts of the building, and one leading to the staircase. So much of the original building has been destroyed that its exact connection with the kitchen cannot now be traced. As a rule this connection was fairly direct to the lower end of the hall.

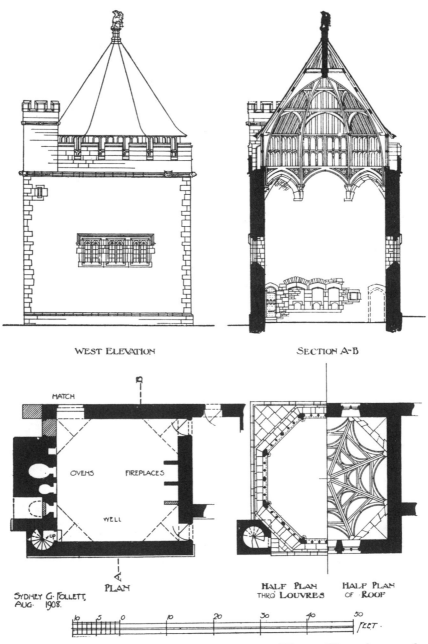

WEST ELEVATION

SECTION A-B

HATCH

OVENS   FIREPLACES

WELL

UP

PLAN

SYDNEY G. FOLLETT,
AUG. 1908.

HALF PLAN
THRO' LOUVRES

HALF PLAN
OF ROOF

10 5 0   10   20   30   40   50
FEET.

32. The Kitchen at Stanton Harcourt—Plans, Elevation, and
Section.

The great kitchen at Burghley House is constructed after the old manner, and is vaulted in stone.   This has led to the statement that it is part of a pre-existing abbey, but there is no reason to suppose that it ante-dates the early parts of the house, which were in building about the year 1550.

There is not much to be said about the other type of kitchen, such as remains at Haddon and South Wingfield.

33. Sketch of the Kitchen at Stanton Harcourt.

It was a large apartment, and usually furnished with several vast fireplaces.   At South Wingfield there were three, two of which are shown in Fig. 34.   At the back of one of these are the two ovens.   None of the examples quoted have windows of any great size, a fact which points to the fire itself having been depended on to supplement the scanty daylight.   As in many other respects so in the kitchens, the great colleges at Oxford and Cambridge afford the best existing illustrations of

E

the internal economy of a mediæval house. They still have to cater for some hundreds of people daily, and so it was in the abbeys and great houses of the Middle Ages. In an abbey kitchen the number for whom cooking was required was sometimes as much as seven or eight hundred. In a nobleman's house, such as Lord Burghley's, the number was less, it is true, but it

34. Fireplaces in the Kitchen, South Wingfield Manor House (*cir.* 1435-40).

must have amounted to one or two hundred. In smaller houses the requirements were not nearly so great, and kitchens of more modest dimensions were sufficient.

CHAPTER V.

THE LATER MANOR HOUSE OF THE MIDDLE AGES.

DURING the fifteenth century a further advance was made in the amenities of house-planning, and although considerable attention was still paid to defensive precautions, there was nevertheless a great expansion in accommodation, and a more determined effort towards obtaining a distinct architectural effect. A certain symmetry of treatment is almost inherent in architecture. It is to be found in the early keeps, where the shallow buttresses or piers and the windows are to a large extent symmetrically placed. But no attempt was made at that time, nor indeed for some centuries, to give a symmetrical disposition to the buildings as a whole. Ranges of rooms were either built entirely new or added to existing buildings as convenience seemed to dictate, and it has already been observed that this haphazard method of planning was extravagant and wasteful. In the fifteenth century there was a noticeable tendency towards symmetry, which easily led in the sixteenth to that very exact balance of part with part so characteristic of the Italian manner, which was to exert an overpowering influence on English designers. Examples of this tendency are to be seen in the beautiful keep at Warkworth in Northumberland (1435-40, Fig. 45, p. 82); in the ruins of Kirby Muxloe in Leicestershire, built by Sir William Hastings about the year 1460 (Figs. 47, 48, pp. 84, 85); and at Cowdray in Sussex, also built in the later years of the same century.

The endeavour to achieve effect by an ordered grouping of the masses of a building is a higher proof of architectural skill than merely to ornament with attractive detail its various parts. Such an attempt, although not very determined, had been made at Kenilworth in the closing years of the fourteenth century. In the fifteenth not only was this idea still further pursued, but a softer and more refined appearance was given to the detail of ornament. The somewhat gaunt character which accorded so well with sterner times often gave way to a pleasant play of fancy, and to that careful and painstaking design which is observable in the Perpendicular style. Men began to desire to have fine houses, the fear of damage and destruction was growing less, and the whole tendency was towards increased refinement. The change is visible in the great manor house of South Wingfield in Derbyshire, where there is not only much charming detail, but an obvious attempt to obtain effect by the handling of masses of building, notably in boldly projecting the *garde-robes* and chimney-stacks from the faces of the walls. Irregularity is still the prevailing characteristic, but among it may be observed a certain striving after rhythmical treatment.

South Wingfield rivals its more famous neighbour, Haddon, in extent; but in some respects it is less interesting, inasmuch as it is more ruinous, and has not the same variety of work to link it up with all periods from the thirteenth century onwards. Wingfield is practically all of one date, having been built by Ralph Cromwell, Lord Treasurer to Henry VI., about 1435-40. A glance at the plan (Fig. 35) shows how ample the accommodation must have been before the house was destroyed. There are two large courts, the outer (or southern), formed of barns, stables, guard-houses and other inferior buildings, the inner (or northern), of the hall, kitchen, and the chambers occupied by the family.

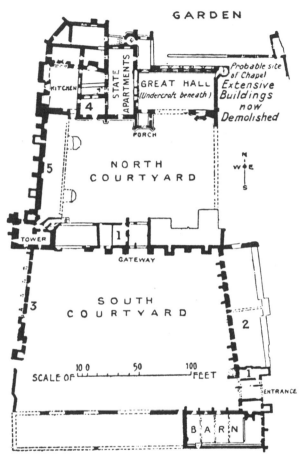

35. South Wingfield Manor House, Derbyshire (*cir.* 1435-40).

Ground Plan.

1, 1. Porter.
2. Guardroom.
3. Site of buildings destroyed.
4. Serving-place.
5. Wing traditionally said to have been occupied by Mary, Queen of Scots.

   The state apartments at the west end of the hall were on the upper floor: on the ground floor were the buttery, passage to kitchen, &c.

This arrangement is an advance in classification, and it is one which controlled the planning of some of the finest of the mansions of the Elizabethan and Jacobean periods. Here, however, the courts are irregular in shape and disposition ; there is no attempt at symmetry, nor much at alignment. The outer court is entered at the south-east corner, and although the gateway to the inner is fairly central, and is placed almost opposite to the porch of the hall, there is little of that accuracy of planning which marks the great houses of a hundred and fifty years later. Some attempt at alignment there is, for standing in the south court, the eye obtains a vista through the large arch of the gatehouse, across the north court, through the porch and the doors beyond, and so on to the distant woods. There is a curious variation from the customary relation of the great hall and kitchens, caused by the insertion on the upper floor of a large state apartment between the hall and the servants' quarters. This is an arrangement not usually found either before or after this period. It does not mark the first step in a new departure. The hall stands on a vaulted undercroft, and must have been a fine room ; it measures 71 ft. 7 in. long by 36 ft. 5 in. wide, and is considerably larger than the hall at Haddon, which is 43 ft. by 28 ft. It is now roofless and ruinous, but the bay window (Fig. 36), and porch, which still survive, are fine examples of late Perpendicular work, as also is the adjacent gable of the state apartment (Fig. 37). There is nothing to indicate where the hall fireplace was situated. The probability is that it was in one of the long side walls, but even as late as a hundred years after this time fires were sometimes placed upon central hearths, and it may have been so here.

The apartments devoted to the use of the family, which we should expect to find at the upper end of the hall (in this case the east end), did in fact once exist, as may be seen by various indications on the building itself and the adjacent ground, but they have all been destroyed, leaving their extent and nature as a matter for conjecture. They were reached by means of the

36. South Wingfield Manor House.

Bay Window of Hall.

circular staircase at the north-east corner of the hall (see plan, Fig. 35), which still retains the doorways that led into them.

The undercroft beneath the hall is one of the finest

pieces of work left (Fig. 38). It is vaulted with heavy
stone ribs springing from columns down the middle,
and responds on the walls. The ribs meet at the summit
on large traceried bosses, and the junction of the

37. South Wingfield Manor House.

Porch of Great Hall and Gable of State Apartments.

ceiling-ribs with the wall-ribs is emphasised in certain
cases by carved grotesques. In spite of the care
bestowed upon the work, there is no reason to suppose
that the undercroft was put to noble uses; it was in all

probability merely a cellar and store place. It is approached from four directions—externally from under the porch, and through the east wall, whence there is easy access to the north-east stair-turret: and internally from one of the rooms beneath the state chamber, and from the bay of the hall (Fig. 39); as the buffet often stood in the hall bay, this staircase gave easy access

38. South Wingfield Manor House.

Undercroft beneath Great Hall.

for replenishing the buffet from the cellar. The kitchen department is well supplied with rooms and with large fireplaces. A straight passage led from the middle of the lower end of the hall direct to the kitchen. It passed beneath the state apartment, and along the side of a small room which was probably the "survaying-place" or serving room, since the wall is pierced with two large openings, through which the dishes would be passed, and thence carried to the hall. The kitchen itself has three huge fireplaces, in two of which there are ovens. In later years it became customary to place the ovens in a room by themselves, called the " pastry."

39. South Wingfield Manor House.

Interior of Bay Window of Hall; showing Door to Undercroft.

Some of the walls and fireplaces in this part of the house are clearly after-insertions, and point to the fact that the original means of cooking were inadequate for the needs of the large household, which found accommodation in the long ranges of rooms most of which are now destroyed.

The wing on the west of the inner court is traditionally assigned to the use of Mary, Queen of Scots, when she was detained in confinement here from 1569 onwards, under the care of George, sixth Earl of Shrewsbury, whose ancestor, the second earl, had purchased the estate from the builder of the house. An interesting light is thrown upon the sanitary habits of the time by the fact that three weeks after her installation at Wingfield she fell ill ; two physicians deputed by the Privy Council reported that the sanitary conditions of her quarters were bad, whereupon her custodian, the Earl of Shrewsbury, retorted that the evil state of her rooms arose from the uncleanly habits of her own retinue. There seems to be little doubt that in Elizabeth's time the care bestowed upon sanitary arrangements was not nearly so great as in the preceding centuries. An examination of house plans of the end of the sixteenth century shows that the isolation of *garde-robes* or the grouping of them together in separate towers was no longer carried out; they were often placed with a view to convenience of access regardless of their unsavoury characteristics. In the case of the particular complaint at Wingfield, however, the inference is that they were not sufficiently convenient for the views of Mary's household, and yet the west wing, which she is said to have occupied, is well furnished with *garde-robes* placed in the large square projections on this face, two in each on each floor.

The gatehouses have each a large and a small archway (Fig. 40), the large one for vehicles, the small for foot passengers. This double archway was now coming into vogue, and was very generally adopted in gatehouses of the fifteenth century. It indicates, among other things, that vehicles had come into more general use. Adjoining the outer gatehouse is a barn, still in excellent preservation, and offering an interesting example of this kind of building.

Although the accommodation at Wingfield is more elaborate than in houses of earlier date, it is still rather roughly and unscientifically thrown together, involving much waste both of space and material. It is also worthy of note that in spite of its great extent and its magnificent rooms, the only staircases were the old-fashioned circular turret stairs of no great diameter. There was indeed as yet no other fashion to follow, for the ancient newel stair held its own until the time of Elizabeth, when it was suddenly and without any transitional form replaced by wide wooden staircases in straight flights. England has no examples of the magnificent development of circular staircases which are to be seen in so many of the great châteaux of France.

Wingfield, it is also to be noted, was carefully built for defence. It stands nearly at the end of a spur of land, and the ground on three of its sides slopes steeply away, rendering access difficult. At the north end, where the ground is in part rather flatter, it is protected by a deep dry moat and a wall. The south side is the most level, and consequently the outer and inferior court was placed on this side. Even supposing that an attacking force gained possession of this court, there was still the mass of its north wing (Fig. 40) between them and the principal part of the house. The only internal communication between the two courts was through an exceedingly narrow doorway leading to a narrow crooked passage. The external walls of the north court are practically devoid of windows on the ground floor; those of the hall and adjoining rooms looked out on to a garden which lay between them and the high wall overhanging the moat. Here, then, as in other houses, the hall was placed in a secure position, and one in which it was possible to make use of large windows. That this part of the house was tolerably secure is proved by the fact that so much of it remains; for when the place was besieged and captured during the Civil Wars, it was the south court through which the breach was made and entrance was effected. It is to the Civil Wars that Wingfield owes its destruction, for, having caused some trouble to the Parliamentary forces, it was ordered to be "slighted," and was so far destroyed as to be rendered uninhabitable. It passed

40. South Wingfield Manor House.
The North Side of South Courtyard.

from the descendants of the Earl of Shrewsbury, and the hall was for a time patched up as a dwelling. Subsequently it was further dismantled in order to build a new house at the foot of the hill. Since then time, as destructive as siege-guns, has wrought further havoc, for no more than "summer's honey breath" can an unprotected building

"hold out
Against the wreckful siege of battering days."

41. Tattershall Castle, Lincolnshire
(*cir.* 1440).

But fortunately in recent years the owners have realised this, and have taken what steps they can to arrest further decay.

Another interesting and remarkable house of this period is Tattershall Castle in Lincolnshire, which was built by the same Lord Treasurer who built Wingfield. In Elizabeth's time several of her great officials built more than one large house, and the fact that Ralph Cromwell did so in the fifteenth century, seems to indicate that house building had already begun to be a pleasure for the great and wealthy, and was not merely undertaken of necessity. It is difficult to say for certain how large the house at Tattershall was originally, or of what its accommodation consisted. There are considerable remains of walls extending over a large area, but the only habitable portion left, if we except the small house now occupied by the caretaker, is the splendid brick tower built after the fashion of a luxurious keep. The reversion to the earlier type is curious, and it seems tolerably certain that, whatever the buildings may have been which have disappeared, the tower was the chief part of the house (Fig. 41). It rises sheer from the ground

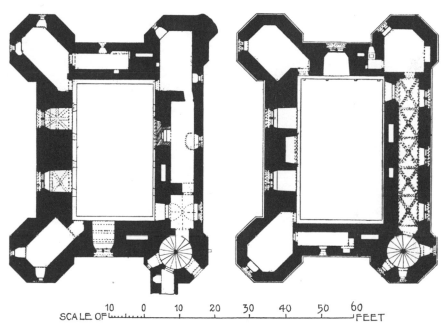

SCALE OF ⌐10 0 10 20 30 40 50 60⌐ FEET

42. Tattershall Castle.
Plans of Second and Third Storeys.

to a vast height—some 120 ft. to the top of the turrets, and more than 100 ft. to the battlements. It can only be called "vast" speaking in terms of English architecture of the time; dwellers in American cities of to-day where buildings soar to 400 ft., would regard it as puny. It contained, in addition to the cellar, four lofty storeys (of which the second and third are shown on Fig. 42), and above them a flat roof with a rampart walk. Each floor consisted of one large room about 38 ft. by 22 ft., supplemented by small chambers in three of the turrets, and by one or two others in the walls, which are some 12 ft. thick.   There are *garde-robes* on each floor (except the first) and on the battlements ; each of the large rooms has a fireplace, and access from floor to floor is obtained by a circular staircase, 10 ft. in diameter.   The rooms are approached from the stairs through vaulted lobbies, and on the third floor through a long vaulted passage in the thickness of the wall.

43. Tattershall Castle.

The Staircase.

The accommodation is of much the same character and extent as in the early keeps, and although the windows are larger, there are but three 'two-light windows to the large rooms, except to that on the ground floor, which has four.   The workmanship is excellent.   The passages and window-recesses are vaulted in brick and are adorned with many shields of arms, as also are the chimney-pieces.   Everything tends to show that the amenities of life were respected, and it is not a little odd that so much care should have been spent upon the embellishment of a dwelling which, although lordly in character, must have been gloomy and uncomfortable, much more so than the spacious manor house at Wingfield.   It is, of course, possible that among the buildings which have disappeared, there may have been more commodious and cheerful rooms, but there is no record of them ; and it is clear from the amount of care spent upon the tower, that it was intended for ordinary occupation.

The jambs of the doors and windows and the tracery of the latter, as well as the machicolations and the coping of the parapet, are all of stone ; so too are the chimney-pieces. But the walls are of brick, and, as already mentioned, so is the vaulting of the passages ; the whole work being a curious mixture of wrought stone and brick. The brick staircase has stone steps and a stone handrail built into the wall (Figs. 43, 44).

The whole place is an interesting example of a reversion to out-of-date arrangements leading back to the past, combined with a desire for beautiful embellishment which points the way to the magnificence which was to become prevalent in the future.

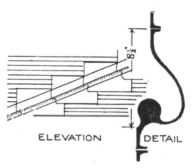

ELEVATION DETAIL

44. Tattershall Castle.
The Stone Handrail.

Another interesting mixture of the ancient and the modern is to be seen at Warkworth Castle in Northumberland. This was a very old foundation retaining much early work in its walls and gatehouse, but about the same time when the Lord Treasurer was building Wingfield, *i.e.*, 1435-40, one of the Percies, Henry, the son of Hotspur, rebuilt the keep at Warkworth. It stands on a steep mound at one end of the castle enclosure, overlooking the little town (Fig. 45). It is planned in the form of a large square with a great bay projecting from the middle of each side, and within this symmetrical outline are ingeniously packed all the rooms which then went to compose a complete house (Fig. 46). It has cellars and a great hall, with buttery and kitchens at one end, while from the other, access is obtained to the chapel and great chamber. On the same floor, occupying odd spaces where they could be contrived, are a few smaller rooms suitable for bedrooms.

45. Warkworth Castle, Northumberland.

The Keep (*cir.* 1435-40).

Numerous small staircases, mostly circular, but some comprised of straight runs in the thickness of the walls, lead up and down in a bewildering fashion. In the centre of the building is an open shaft giving a modicum of light and air to the adjacent rooms. The whole building is a triumph of ingenuity, but a glance at the plan shows that the lighting must have been bad; the great hall, for instance, has only two windows on an outside wall (one being over the fireplace), and one, almost valueless, into the central shaft; the kitchen has but one. It is not therefore surprising to find that after some thirty years had elapsed, a new great hall and kitchen were erected on another part of the

46. Warkworth Castle, Northumberland.

Plan of the Keep.

1. Vestibule (leading from en-   3. Chapel.
     trance in basement).   4. Great chamber.
2. Hall.   5. Kitchens.
             6. Pantry and buttery.

castle close. Most of these latter buildings have perished, but enough remains to show that this second hall had the large windows of the late Perpendicular period, and must consequently have been a far more cheerful apartment than anything in the keep.

The "worm-eaten hold of ragged stone," as Rumour designates Warkworth Castle in the Second Part of

King Henry IV., hardly deserves that description so far as the keep is concerned, for the stonework is in a state of excellent preservation, and the lion of the Percies is still rampant in full vigour high up on the wing facing the town. The view (Fig. 45) indicates how careful the builders were to place no large windows near the ground, while showing at the same time that they paid great attention to the appearance and careful execution of their design. The side illustrated faces into the

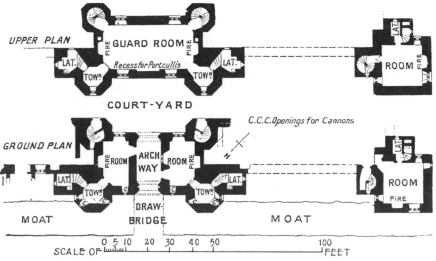

47. Kirby Muxloe, Leicestershire (*cir.* 1460).

Plans of remaining Buildings.

castle yard, where most secure from attack, and is more cheerfully lighted than those which face the town. It is obvious in all these illustrations of fifteenth-century buildings that the old haphazard methods are gradually giving way to a desire for more rhythmical arrangement.

One of the last houses to be built with any serious intention to have it strongly fortified must have been the "Castle" at Kirby Muxloe in Leicestershire, of which some interesting ruins remain. It was surrounded by a moat, and had a gateway protected by a drawbridge, a portcullis, and two projecting towers (Fig. 47). The recess into which the drawbridge fitted when drawn up, is plainly visible (Fig. 48) as are the holes in the wall through which the chains worked.   When thus elevated it completely closed the gateway.   Behind it was the portcullis which slid up and down in a groove.   There is a recess in the wall of the room over the gateway into which it fitted when raised.   The projecting towers are furnished with circular openings of about 6 in. diameter

48. Kirby Muxloe.   The Entrance Gateway.

for the purpose of admitting the muzzle of a cannon, thus replacing the long vertical openings or oillets which were in vogue when arrows were the principal missiles. There are not many examples of such provision for the use of artillery, but among them may be mentioned Hurstmonceux Castle in Sussex, of about the same date.

The remains are not extensive, but they are enough to show that the building was arranged with strict symmetry round a courtyard (Fig. 49); another curious instance of the mixture of ancient methods of defence with modern effort after architectural effect. The chief material employed is brick, but the dressings are of stone with bold, simple mouldings. Ornament is very sparingly introduced; there are indications of diaper work in darker bricks, and these are also employed to trace a heraldic maunch in the walls of the towers, this being the cognizance of the Sir William Hastings who built the castle about the year 1460. Owing to its ruinous condition the place throws but little light on the domestic arrangements of the times. The gate-house was clearly occupied by the guards; the corner tower evidently contained living rooms; both buildings are well supplied with latrines, or *garde-robes*. In all probability the great hall stood in the side opposite to the entrance. The chief interest of the house lies in its symmetrical plan and in its well-marked means of defence.

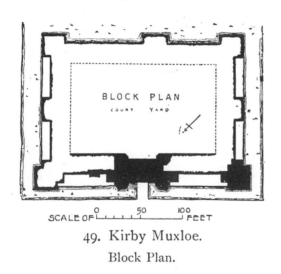

49. Kirby Muxloe.
Block Plan.

With the close of the fifteenth century the necessity for anything like strong fortification disappeared; a new era was approaching in which men were to build for pleasure, comfort, cheerfulness, magnificence. The dark ages were past, the Renaissance was at hand. This, therefore, will be a convenient point at which to break off for a time the story of the growth of the house, and turn our attention to some of the features which lend interest to such dwellings as we have been considering.

CHAPTER VI.

MEDIÆVAL DOMESTIC FEATURES — DOORWAYS, WINDOWS, FIREPLACES, CHIMNEYS, ROOFS AND CEILINGS, STAIRCASES.

THE treatment of special features in domestic buildings was (as already pointed out) generally simpler than that of similar features in churches, although it followed much the same lines in both cases. On the whole, such things as doorways, windows, fireplaces, roofs and ceilings were handled in houses with much simplicity during the prevalence of the Gothic or mediæval styles. In this respect they present a striking contrast to the elaboration bestowed upon them in later years when houses were built for comfort and splendour, and when a study of the methods of the artists of the Renaissance enabled our English designers to indulge in determined efforts at magnificent design.

It may be that in house-building the work was purposely subordinated to that adopted in church-building: it may be that the fact of houses being subject to attacks from which the sacred character of churches preserved them, led to an avoidance of costly or elaborate ornament. But, whatever the reason, the richest of domestic doorways and windows cannot compare in splendour with the finer specimens of such features in churches or cathedrals; and, as a rule, their richness was restrained within severe and narrow bounds. In some of the more important dwellings, especially in the earliest times, considerable attention was bestowed upon doorways, and the employment of several " orders," or shallow arches placed in receding fashion one behind the other, led to striking and even noble effects. Windows are such vulnerable points that they were in early times almost always small and plain.   Ceilings were merely the constructional expression of the floors of which they formed the under side.   Fireplaces were

50. Warkworth Castle.
Entrance Gateway (late 14th cent.).

only so far ornamented as their construction seemed to suggest, especially in the earlier examples. It was not until the time of Elizabeth that the chimney-piece as a stately and predominating feature came into fashion.

During the mediæval period, throughout the whole of which it was necessary to guard against assault, EXTERNAL DOORWAYS were simple in treatment, and

were protected either by being placed in a recess com-
manded by openings through which arrows could be
shot (called oillets), or by being surmounted at greater
or less height by projecting stonework which concealed
openings (called machicolations) through which missiles
of various kinds could be hurled upon the heads of those
attempting to force an entrance. In many cases, as at
Warkworth Castle (Fig. 50), both these methods of

a   *b*

51. Doorways.

(*a*) From Prebendal House, Nassington, Northamptonshire.
(*b*) Doorway (right) and Window (left), Rochester Castle, Kent (*c.* 1130).

defence were adopted. An oillet can be seen on the
canted face to the left of the doorway; the machicolations are carried across between the two turrets.
Frequently the entrance was further protected by
a portcullis, or massive grille of wood, which slid
up and down in a groove in the stonework. Nearly
every castle and many of the fortified houses were
thus defended, and there are innumerable instances in
which the grooves may still be seen. These defensive

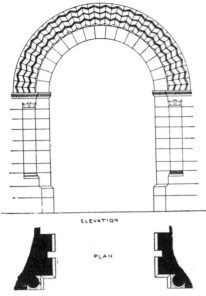

ELEVATION

PLAN

52. Hedingham Castle, Essex.

Entrance Doorway,
with grooves for portcullis.

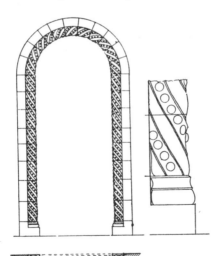

IN 6 0 1 2 3 FEET
1 2 3 4 5 6 7 8 9 10 11 12 INCHES

53. Hedingham Castle.
(*cir.* 1130).

Archway from Stairs to Gallery.

arrangements are an interesting subject, but are outside the present purpose, except in so far as they affect the architectural treatment. Machicolations are sometimes found over doors in dwelling-houses, but more generally in connection with the gatehouse. They not infrequently occur at the summit of towers, and impart the characteristic appearance produced by the heavy projection which they necessitated. One result of the universal need for protection was that doorways were generally small; small, that is, in comparison with those that came into use in the seventeenth century. Even the principal doors of a house were restricted in size, and were generally in one sheet, not divided down the middle and hung on either hand. The commonest form of fastening was a stout oak bar, which when out of use was pushed back into a long recess in the wall, and when wanted was drawn across the door far enough for its end to fit into a shallow recess in the opposite jamb.

Early doorways are usually round-headed; sometimes the sweep of the arch was not fully semicircular but segmental. In important buildings like Rochester Castle and Hedingham, the arches were either of several orders or were richly ornamented with the zigzag or spiral mouldings characteristic of the period (Figs. 51, 52, 53). In houses of less importance, such as the prebendal house at Nassington, the treatment was simpler (Fig. 51*a*). In this case, although the arch is round, the label terminations show it to be of somewhat later date, probably early in the thirteenth century, or nearly a hundred years after those at Rochester and Hedingham.

54. Aydon Castle, Northumberland
(*cir.* 1280).

Doorway to Hall.

Early in the thirteenth century arches became pointed, and doorways followed suit; accordingly the example from Aydon Castle in Northumberland (*c.* 1280), shows the later form (Fig. 54). It is a good instance of the very general practice of entering the upper floor through an external door approached by

55. Bishop's Palace, Mayfield, Sussex.
Doorway to Hall (early 14th cent.)

a flight of steps. The marks where the protecting roof abutted against the wall are plainly visible. As this doorway opened from an interior courtyard, special measures of defence were not considered necessary. Of still later date is the doorway of the Bishop's palace at Mayfield, in Sussex (Fig. 55). This charming little drawing not only shows the unusually wide doorway, but also affords a glimpse into the great hall, with its Decorated window and the springing of one of the stone arches

56. Northborough Manor House, Northamptonshire.
Doorways in the Screens (mid. 14th cent.).

57.

(*a*) Norrington Wilts (late 14th cent.).
(*b*) Eltham Palace, Kent (15th cent.).
(*c*) Lenham, Kent (late 15th cent.).
(*d*) Lacock, Wiltshire; from the Angel Inn (early 16th cent.).

which carried the roof timbers.   The Decorated period delighted in ogee arches, ball-flowers, and crockets, and it bestowed them upon the three doorways at North-borough (Fig. 56), which led from the screens of the hall to the buttery, kitchen, and pantry. The illustration is sketched from a point within the screens, and shows the inside of the front door on the extreme right.   The manor house at Northborough is of very considerable interest in spite of the alterations which have been found necessary to adapt it to modern uses.   It retains its old hall, now divided into two storeys ; and the rather elaborate tracery of its windows can still be detected, although built up in order to accommodate the inserted floor.

58. Doorway from Harrietsham, Kent (late 15th cent.).

The house is approached across a court into which access is obtained through a vaulted gatehouse, which has suffered much mutilation.   Most of the other buildings which form the court are of the seventeenth century, and the whole group is full of the suggestions prompted by time-worn buildings, especially where they reveal themselves to the traveller in some remote village.   It became customary in the Perpendicular period to surround the pointed arch with a rectangular frame, as shown in the various examples in Fig. 57. The first step is taken in the doorway at Norrington in Wiltshire; the idea is more resolutely carried out in the others. The Norrington archway is boldly moulded, and it leads into a vaulted porch, a feature less fre- quently found in houses than in churches. The doorway from El- tham Palace has the spandrels, formed by the curved arch and the rectangular frame, filled with tracery, and it is surmounted by a bold square- headed label. The Lacock example shows a later type, in which the pointed head is flattened in the manner custom- ary in Tudor times, a manner which lingered on,

59. Eastington Hall, Worcestershire.
Entrance Doorway (late 15th cent.).

with variations, until well into the reign of James I. The fourth example, from Lenham, is of wood, unlike the others, which are of stone. It shows that the same treatment was applied to both materials alike. There is another good example of a late doorway in wood at Harrietsham, in Kent (Fig. 58). This sketch is valuable

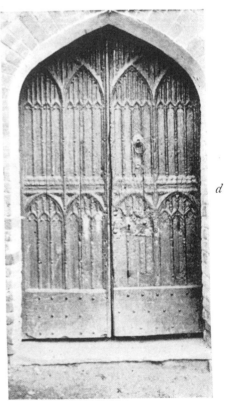

60.

(a) Doorway of Porch, Wingfield Manor Derbyshire (1435-40).
(b) Door from Hall to Garden, Wingfield Manor.
(c) Door in "Pope's Tower," Stanton Harcourt, Oxfordshire (late 15th cent.).
(d) Door to School, Ewelme, Oxfordshire (cir. 1440).

as affording a glimpse into the screens of the hall, with doorways on the right, leading to the servants' quarters. The doorway from the excellent half-timber house at Eastington, in Worcestershire, is another good example in wood (Fig. 59). The beautiful doorways from South Wingfield (Fig. 60, *a*, *b*) are specimens of the best work of the Perpendicular period: that from Stanton Harcourt (Fig. 60, *c*) is a good example of a small stone doorway with its original oak door and iron hinges; it has a worthy companion in the little door at Lacock. The last example in Fig. 60, *d*, shows a more elaborately designed oak door from the school at Ewelme in Oxfordshire. The fittings of the doors are worthy of attention; the wood handle and iron knocker at Lenham, the knocker at Lacock, and the wood bolt at Stanton Harcourt.

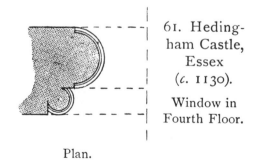

Plan.

61. Hedingham Castle, Essex (*c.* 1130).

Window in Fourth Floor.

When the doorways were of stone, the doors were not hung in wood frames, but on stout hooks let into the stonework. It was impossible, therefore, to shut them tight; there was always space enough between the door and the stone to admit draughts and copious piles of snow. In later years, as we shall see, door frames become universal, but if found in mediæval houses they may be regarded as insertions, unless the whole construction is of wood as in the examples from Lenham and Harrietsham.

WINDOWS.—In all early houses the windows were small, owing to the necessity for defence. On the ground floor they were little more than narrow slits, three or four inches wide; but in the rooms less directly exposed to attack, they were somewhat enlarged, although still far short in area of the minimum required by modern by-laws, namely, one-tenth of the floor space. They were unglazed, except in important houses, such as those belonging to the king. Indeed, examples are not infrequent, even in the fifteenth century, of windows never having been glazed. Sheets of horn were sometimes used in order to keep out the wind, without absolutely excluding the light. From the earliest times windows were closed by shutters, which sometimes covered the whole window, when it was not too large; and sometimes were provided for each subdivision; for as already remarked, domestic windows were often

62. Chacombe Priory.
Window (late 12th cent.).

63. Alnwick Castle, Northumberland.

Window (13th cent.), showing Window-seats and Recesses for Shutters.
The glazing is of later date.

a

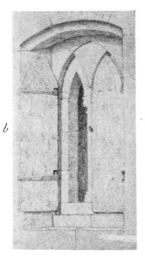

b

64. Little Wenham Hall, Suffolk (13th cent.).

(*a*) Window on Upper Floor.
(*b*) Window between Hall and Chapel.

65. South Wingfield Manor.

Window in Porch (1435-40.)

divided by crossbars or transomes in order to obtain lights of reasonable size in regard to the shutters. Tracery was sparingly employed, and was usually not covered by the shutters; the openings thus left formed useful outlets for the smoke, but must have been considered by reflecting minds to be only a crude method of ventilation.

The treatment of house windows corresponded with that adopted in churches. First they were round-headed, as at Castle Hedingham (Fig. 61), and Rochester (Fig. 51, *b*). Then they became pointed, with, perhaps, a dividing mullion, as at Little Wenham Hall (Fig. 64, *b*). The plain pointed heads were then bent into a trefoil shape, as at Chacombe Priory (Fig. 62), or were made with a flat summit and curved shoulders, as at Alnwick Castle (Fig. 63). Tracery

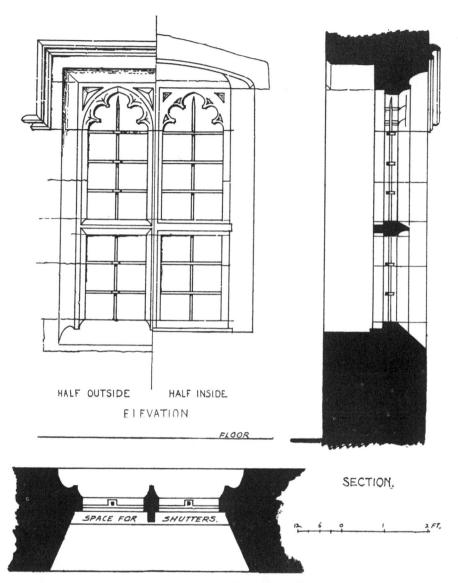

HALF OUTSIDE   HALF INSIDE.

ELEVATION

FLOOR

SECTION.

SPACE FOR   SHUTTERS.

66. Abingdon Abbey, Berkshire.

Window in Guest-house (late 15th cent.).

was occasionally introduced, as at Little Wenham
(Fig. 64, *a*). This illustration and that from Chacombe,
as well as the view of Oakham Castle (Fig. 15), show
that the forerunner of the mullion was a shaft dividing

67. Brympton D'Evercy, Somerset.
Bay Window (late 15th cent.).

68. Fawsley, Northamptonshire.
Bay Window of the Hall (late 15th cent.).

the lights. In subsequent examples the mullion will be found fully established.

The stone window frame itself was placed at the outside face of the wall, and as the latter was of great thickness, the space inside was furnished with stone seats, which are well shown in the example from Alnwick Castle (Fig. 63), where also the sinking to contain the shutters is plainly visible. The shutter itself is shown in the Little Wenham example (Fig. 64, b), and in the window at Stokesay (Fig. 23). The glazing of all these windows may be considered as inserted in later years; but whether glazed or not, the lights were pro-

tected by iron bars down to the end of the sixteenth
century.

A Decorated window of the fourteenth century is
given in the illustration from the palace at Mayfield
(Fig. 55), and again in that of Penshurst (Fig. 71).
The charming window from the porch at South Wingfield of the Perpendicular period (Fig. 65), has unusually
elaborate tracery, but it serves to emphasise the resemblance between domestic and ecclesiastical architecture,
as also do the larger windows from the same house—the
bay, and the window in the gable of the state apartment
shown in Figs. 36 and 37.

An excellent example of the late fifteenth century is
to be seen at Abingdon Abbey, in the very interesting
guest-house (Fig. 66). These lights were not glazed, but
were furnished with iron bars and shutters. During the
fifteenth century, owing to the less urgent need for
defence, windows increased in size, and by the end of
that century windows of six or eight lights, or even long
ranges of lights, were not infrequent.

One of the most striking features of domestic architecture, and one which in the hands of Elizabethan
designers often dominated the composition of their
façades, was the BAY WINDOW. By the later architects
it was repeated symmetrically so as to help the rhythm
of the design. But in mediæval times, with which we
are now dealing, it was treated as an isolated feature,
and was seldom used except to add to the amenities of
the daïs in the great hall. In this position it gave a little
extra space, conveniently situated for the reception of a
sideboard. Its lights were brought down low enough
to afford an outlook, whereas the other windows of the
hall were kept up some 10 or 12 ft. from the floor. Even
when used singly and without any idea of symmetrical
repetition, the bay window was a commanding feature,

and was frequently the occasion of such happy archi-
tectural grouping as may be seen at Brympton
D'Evercy, in Somerset
(Fig. 67).

It is not easy to say
when bay windows were
first introduced, but ap-
parently not earlier than
the middle of the four-
teenth century; they were,
however, generally adopted
during the fifteenth, and
the Perpendicular style
affords many beautiful
examples. Among them
may be mentioned South
Wingfield (Fig. 36), and
Fawsley in Northampton-
shire (Fig. 68). The ceilings of these bays were
not infrequently vaulted
in stone, with elaborate
tracery and cusps, as is
the case in this fine window at Fawsley, the
Deanery at Wells, the oriel
at Great Chalfield in Wiltshire, and many others.
The great bay at Fawsley
is of unusual interest, inasmuch as there is a small
chamber above it, which
was originally approached
by a narrow newel staircase.   Owing to its remote
position, tradition has assigned this chamber as the

69. Sherborne, Dorset.
Oriel Window (15th cent.).

secret place where the celebrated Martin Marprelate tracts were printed.

Bay windows were occasionally introduced on an upper floor, being corbelled out from the face of the wall; such windows are called oriels. There is a good example at Sherborne in Dorset, of Perpendicular date (Fig. 69). The earliest known example of an oriel window is at Prudhoe Castle, in Northumberland; it is

70. Glastonbury, Somerset.
Front of Wood House, showing Window and Doors.

not actually corbelled out, however, but rests on a cross-wall below.

The construction of wooden houses, formed of stout uprights placed at short intervals, lent itself freely to the introduction of long ranges of window lights such as those in a street front at Glastonbury (Fig. 70), where the framing of the walls served also as the frame of the window.

FIREPLACES occur in some of the earliest buildings; that is, large recesses specially contrived in the walls, with an outlet for the smoke carried up for some distance in the masonry. This arrangement appears to have been adopted very generally, and was by no means a luxury of later times. It is true that the alternative method of a central hearth in the middle of the floor was also of frequent occurrence. But both ways of heating were in vogue at the same time. The wall fireplace is not the successor of the central hearth, but if anything its predecessor. When it is remembered that in the early keeps the various rooms were placed one over the other, it is clear that the facilities for the escape of smoke from the lower rooms would have been but small had the fire been on a central hearth. There would indeed have been no exits for it but the small windows. Accordingly most keeps are provided with fireplaces in the walls. A good example is furnished at Castle Hedingham (Fig. 6). On the other hand, in the great halls of the fortified manor houses, which were usually of one storey, it was an easy matter to contrive an opening in the roof immediately over the central hearth. This opening was protected by a ventilating turret called the louvre, which kept off the rain, but allowed the smoke—or as much of it as was not wafted about the room—to escape through it. As the roofs were constructed of wood, so too of necessity was the louvre, and owing to the lapse of time and to other destructive agencies, both roofs and louvres of the early periods have perished. In some houses, such as Stokesay, the central hearth of the great hall still remains, while in the smaller rooms fireplaces of contemporary date are also to be seen. It is clear that the central hearth was not considered an intolerable nuisance, inasmuch as it survived until the end of the fifteenth century and later : the great hall at Richmond Palace, built for Henry VII., had one ; so too had Deene Hall, already referred to, which was built in the reign of

71. Penshurst Place, Kent.

The Great Hall.

72. Abingdon Abbey, Berkshire.

Chimney-shaft and Chimney-vent (13th cent.).

Edward VI. The louvre for the central hearth had a direct successor in the lantern light so often seen in Georgian houses; the connection between the two may be seen in some of the halls of the colleges at Oxford and Cambridge, where it is evident that the lantern light stands in the same place as the ancient louvre, and is but a modernised version of that feature. An excellent example of a central hearth in a great hall may still be seen at Penshurst Place in Kent (Fig. 71). This, although of later date, about 1350, is typical of all such cases.

73. Abingdon Abbey.
Orifice of Chimney-vent.

Although the early keeps were usually warmed (if warmed it may be called) by fireplaces, there are exceptions such as the Peak Castle, where there are no signs of such accommodation. How these places were heated is not apparent, but as flues of lath and plaster were occasionally used, and the hoods of fireplaces were sometimes formed of wood, it is probable that a perishable expedient of this nature was adopted.

CHIMNEYS.—It has already been pointed out that in quite early times, as at Castle Hedingham, the fire-

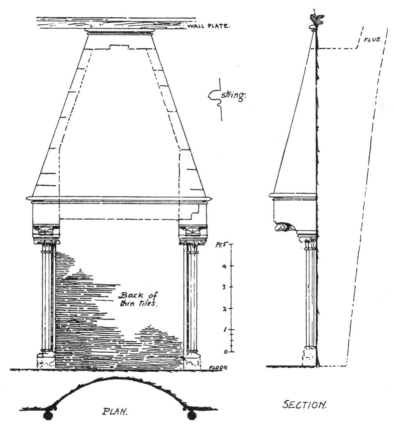

74. Abingdon Abbey, Berkshire.

Fireplace (13th cent.).

place flue was not carried up to any great height, but was shortly conducted to an orifice in the face of the wall (see Fig. 6). There is a fireplace of even earlier date, similarly contrived, at Colchester Castle. It is doubtful whether any example of a chimney-shaft of

Norman times is to be found. One of the earliest remaining chimney-shafts is at Abingdon Abbey on the Thames in Berkshire (Fig. 72), a well-known river landmark. The large square stack contains a single flue, which rises from the fireplace of the upper room, and delivers its smoke through the vertical openings at the summit. In the fireplace of the lower room the earlier method was adopted, and the smoke emerged from the little projection in the wall to the left of the base of the large stack : a plan of the orifice is given in Fig. 73. The date of this work is about the middle of the thirteenth century. The fireplace which is served by the large flue is shown in Fig. 74.

75. Stokesay Castle, Shropshire.

Fireplace in North Tower (13th cent.).

Of much the same date are the fireplaces at Stokesay, of one of which the remains are shown in Fig. 75. The wooden kerb or frame supported by the corbels appears to be of the original date, and must have carried a wooden hood. But as a rule these hoods were of stone as at Abingdon Abbey. The earliest fireplaces were flush with the wall, but it was soon found necessary to introduce a projecting hood in order to catch the smoke —a contrivance familiar to us, though on a small scale, in many modern fire-grates.

A sort of compromise between a wall orifice and a chimney-shaft is to be seen at Aydon Castle (Fig. 76), where there are also several simple fireplaces with stone hoods, of about 1280 (Fig. 77, *a*, *b*). The wall orifice was, no doubt, found to be insufficient for its purpose, and the chimney-shaft was further developed. It should be borne in mind that not every room was provided with a fireplace; consequently the chimney-shafts were nearly always isolated features; chimney-stacks

76. Aydon Castle, Northumberland.
Chimney-shaft (*cir.* 1280).

combining several flues grouped together followed in later years, when it became customary to warm more rooms.

As in all other mediæval work, the ornamental treatment of chimneys varied with the changes of style.   Of

a

c

b

d

77. Fireplaces.

(*a*, *b*) From Aydon Castle (*cir*. 1240).
(*c*) From Sherborne Abbey (15th cent.).
(*d*) From the Church House, Salisbury (15th cent.).

the late Decorated period is that at Northborough (Fig. 78); of yet later date are those in the Vicar's Close at Wells (Fig. 79), and that at Harringworth (Fig. 80).

Fireplaces in the meanwhile changed with the progress of years. The hood which had been adopted in order to catch the smoke when the recess for the fire was shallow, was in turn aban-

78. Northborough, Northamptonshire.

Chimney (14th cent.).

79. Vicar's Close, Wells

Chimney (15th cent.).

doned when the recess was made deeper, and it became no longer necessary. The hoods had been rather plain, gaunt features, devoid of superfluous ornament. As the amenities of life increased with the diminishing need of defensive precautions, so also did the desire for embellishment, and during the Perpendicular period, a great amount of attention was bestowed upon the decoration of fireplaces. The stone work which surrounded the recess was panelled and cusped, and enclosed

H

by shafts supporting a cornice—the forerunner of our familiar chimney shelf (Fig. 77, *c, d*). Heraldry began to play an important part in the decoration. At Aydon may be seen (Fig. 77, *a*) the first uncertain step in the direction to which Tattershall (Figs. 81, 82) and Fawsley (Fig. 83) subsequently led. The richness to which the fifteenth century attained was, however, far outdone by that which the Elizabethan designers achieved a century later.

80. Harringworth, Northamptonshire.

Chimney (15th cent.).

There are no remains extant of quite early domestic ROOFS OR CEILINGS; but from the appearance of the stone walls, it is tolerably certain that they were built of wood. Stone vaulting very seldom occurs except in a few rooms on the ground floor, and in such cases it was probably adopted as a safeguard against fire. The little keep or tower at Longthorpe in Northamptonshire has its ground floor stone-vaulted: so, too, have many of the peel-towers of Northumberland. But the great keeps at Rochester, Hedingham, and elsewhere, had roofs and floors of wood. The huge beams which carried the floors no doubt showed in the room below, but there is no evidence that in early times any special attention

81. Tattershall Castle, Lincolnshire.

Chimney-piece on Upper Floor, showing Heraldic Decoration.

82. Tattershall Castle, Lincolnshire.

Chimney-piece on Ground Floor (1430-40).

was devoted to ornamenting the ceiling.   In the fifteenth
century the constructional beams were moulded and
arranged with some regularity, as plenty of examples
prove ; and this, if any, was probably the method adopted
in early times.

The great halls of manor houses, which, as already
said, were usually
of one storey, were
covered with fine
open timber roofs,
and although no
early examples
are left, there are
plenty of the
fifteenth century
and even earlier.
The construction
of such roofs is
probably more or
less familiar to
most people. The
outer covering of
lead, slates, or
tiles rested on the
rafters, which
were supported
on longitudinal
beams called pur-
lins ; these in
their turn were carried by strongly framed supports called principals (*i.e.*, principal rafters), which
spanned the hall from side to side at intervals
of twelve feet or thereabouts.   Sometimes, though
rarely, as at Mayfield Palace (Fig. 55) and Ightham Mote in Kent, the principal was a great stone

83. Fawsley, Northamptonshire.

Chimney-piece in Great Hall (15th cent.).

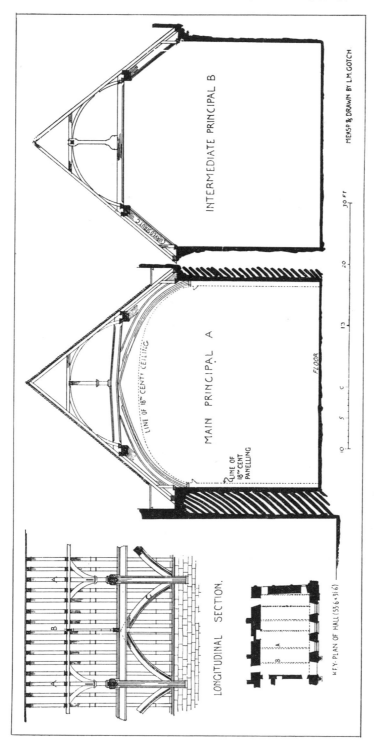

84. Drayton House, Northamptonshire.
Roof of the Great Hall (*cir.* 1328).

arch.*   But as a rule, it was of massive timber framed together, and it was in the construction of this feature that the most obvious opportunities for ornamental

85. Little Sodbury, Gloucestershire.

Roof of Hall (15th cent.).

treatment occurred.   In churches it was carried occa-

* See the *Transactions of the Royal Institute of British Architects*, vol. v., New Series, for an interesting conjectural restoration of the Mayfield roof by Mr G. E. Street, R.A.

sionally to the most astonishing lengths; but in houses this exuberance was restrained, and as a rule the open timber roofs of houses, although extremely handsome, were quite soberly treated. A fairly early example of the thirteenth century is to be seen at Stokesay (Fig. 20). Of the fourteenth century may be

86. Eltham Palace, Kent.

Roof of Great Hall (late 15th cent.).

mentioned Drayton House in Northamptonshire (Fig. 84), now quite hidden by a ceiling of much later years, and Penshurst Place (Fig. 71). Of the fifteenth century is Little Sodbury (Fig. 85), while of the late fifteenth is Eltham Palace (Fig. 86).

The Drayton example is interesting inasmuch as there are two types of principal: the main principals

87. Crowhurst Place, Surrey.
Ceiling with Moulded Beams.

carry the pur-
lins, which in
their turn carry
the intermedi-
ates; they are
strengthened
and supported
where this ad-
ditional load
comes, by curved
braces or struts,
which rest on
the wall at the
foot of the
main principals.

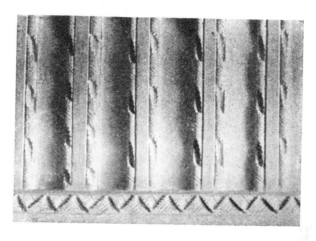

88. Lavenham, Suffolk.

Ceiling with Carved Beams.

Curved braces were very commonly employed; they

89. Lyddington, Rutland.

Hall of Bede House, showing Panelled
Wood Ceiling and Traceried Cornice
(early 16th cent.).

occur both at Little
Sodbury and El-
tham, and in the
latter case the
curves are so de-
signed as to form a
feature in the de-
corative effect. In
this example it will
be seen that a more
determined effort at
design has been
made, the whole
work has been more
carefully thought
out than in the
others. It is, more-
over, of the hammer-
beam type; that is,

the main arch of the principal does not spring from the wall itself, but from a projecting piece of timber (the hammer-beam), which is supported by a curved strut springing from the wall.

The open timber roof survived in places down to the early years of the seventeenth century. But the fashion of having lofty halls then gradually fell into disuse; halls were surmounted by a room above them, and the need for a handsome roof disappeared, its place being taken by a flat, decorated ceiling.

90. Lavenham, Suffolk.

Part of Panelled Ceiling, showing Boss at the Junction of the Wood Ribs (early 16th cent.).

Ceilings, such as we conceive the word, were not known in mediæval work, at any rate not until late in the fifteenth century. The ceiling was, in fact, the underside of the floor above, and its ornamental character was obtained by a regular disposition of the constructional timbers, and by working mouldings on the latter. The effect was massive and handsome, the ceiling (for want of a better word) being divided into large deeply recessed squares or oblongs by heavily moulded beams. Crowhurst Place in Surrey has a good example of this treatment (Fig. 87). In some instances the underside of the floor joists (*i.e.*, the smaller timbers which rested on the beams and carried the floor boards) was carved, as in the curious example from a house at Lavenham in Suffolk (Fig. 88).

The origin of the ceiling as distinguished from the underside of the floor, appears to be found late in the fifteenth century, or early in the sixteenth, when the practice was introduced of covering the lower sides of the floor joists with flat boarding and dividing the level surface into panels by means of applied mouldings. Such a ceiling is found in the Bede House at Lyddington in Rutland, formerly a country house of the Bishops of Lincoln (Fig. 89). The junction of the ribs was sometimes ornamented with a carved boss such as is shown

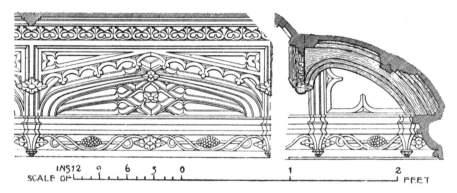

91. Lyddington Bede House.

Traceried Cornice in Wood.

in Fig. 90, also from a house in Lavenham. This simple method of treating ceilings was developed in course of time into the elaborate plasterwork of Elizabethan houses. The room at Lyddington has a very remarkable wood cornice fashioned after the manner of the fan tracery prevalent at the end of the fifteenth century (Fig. 91). But this kind of ornament was not at all general, and it may be doubted whether any other instance of it can be cited.

STAIRCASES.—There is little to be said about

mediæval staircases. They were almost universally of the corkscrew type, the steps winding round a central newel, as at Tattershall Castle (Fig. 43). There was but little opportunity for embellishment, and accordingly none is to be found, the nearest approach being the treatment of the stone handrail already shown in Fig. 44. The steps were usually of stone, the undersides being sloped off to afford as much head room as possible below them. In some instances when the summit of the staircase was reached, the roof of the enclosure was vaulted with some attention to appearances, but beyond this the ornamental treatment did not go. There are a few instances of these staircases being vaulted all the way up in brick, the steps themselves being then built up on the top of the vaulting. This was a clever and ingenious piece of brickwork, but was not especially ornamental. Indeed we have to wait until the time of Elizabeth for any display of fancy in the treatment of staircases; up to that time they were strictly utilitarian in character.

The WALLS of mediæval houses were frequently left bare, but when they were covered three methods seem to have been adopted. The earliest was to apply a thin layer of plaster, a method which has survived to the present day. But whereas nowadays the plaster is of sufficient thickness to cover all the irregularities of the wall and to be brought to a perfectly true and even surface, in early times it was quite thin, and although it stopped all the crevices, it retained the main irregularities of the wall, and produced a pleasant variety of effect. The plaster was frequently decorated with coloured lines or simple patterns, and occasionally with figure subjects. The next method was to cover the walls with wainscot, that is, with oak panelling. Of this treatment few, if any, examples survive; but, judging from other

Gothic woodwork, the panels must have been of considerable size set in framing of large scantling. This
work was also frequently painted in colours and patterns.
The third method and the last in point of date, was to
cover them with hangings—tapestry or arras, as they
were generally called, from the town where they were
chiefly manufactured—"the costly cloths of Arras and
of Tours," as Spenser calls them.

CHAPTER VII.

Early Sixteenth Century—Coming of the Italian Influence.

It was during the sixteenth century that took place the most remarkable development in domestic architecture which occurred in England until the middle of the nineteenth century; and especially during the second half was this extraordinary advance particularly noticeable. Several causes produced this effect, chief among them being that great upheaval in thought which gave rise to the wonderful movement known as the Renaissance. The Renaissance stands not only for a revival of ancient forms in architecture, sculpture, and painting, but for a vast awakening in all departments of human enterprise, and the final abandonment of mediævalism with all its crude and crabbed methods and ways of thought. New ways were followed in science, in learning, in religion, in art; and the knowledge of these new ways was widely disseminated by the new invention of printing. So far as architecture was concerned, Italy was the fountain-head of the new stream of thought; and so far as England was concerned, it was in the reign of Henry VIII. that the stream first reached our shores, and affected our traditional methods of design.

The dissolution of the monasteries was another cause of the change which came over building, inasmuch as it transferred into private and secular hands much of the vast possessions hitherto held by the Church. The confusion into which religion was thrown put an effectual stop to church building, and consequently opened the way to increased house building. The abatement of civil strife and the general security of life and property under the strong and sagacious rule of Elizabeth was a further inducement towards the erection of comfortable homes. The rise of the new nobility which sprang from her recognition of talent in persons of comparatively obscure origin, led to the founding of some of the finest houses of which the country can boast. Finally, the desire for magnificence, which has already been noticed in a few instances in the preceding century, became general, fostered as it was by rivalry, the possession of wealth, and the sense of security from internecine strife.

Italy, being the home of the new manner in art, communicated her methods in course of time to her neighbours. Out of her superabundant craftsmen she spared some for other lands. They settled in France, they settled in England ; at least they hardly settled here, but they visited us for longer or shorter periods, and left us a legacy in design. Our own craftsmen gradually, and with some reluctance, adopted their methods, and having become accustomed to the strange forms brought from the far south, they turned in later years with increased eagerness to their near neighbours the Dutch, who had themselves learnt the new lesson in their own stolid and unimaginative way.

The early steps in the change of design are of great interest. They appear at first infrequently and tentatively in insignificant ornament ; then rather more freely ; after a time they affect prominent features such as cornices ; then the pediment appears ; the pointed arch gives way to the semicircular, windows become square-headed ; classic pilasters are introduced, sparingly at first, but afterwards with more freedom ; symmetry of disposition in the plan of the house becomes more frequent. Yet beneath all these Italian adornments the body of the house is of the old English type; with all its foreign variations, the melody itself is native. It is an endless delight to watch the struggles of the English craftsman with his novel ornament. Sometimes they resulted in quaint applications of misunderstood features; sometimes in proportions which would have pained the eye of Palladio; but frequently in charming little bits of design, refreshingly simple and unobtrusive.

Meantime the plan of the house was continued on the old lines, and Henry VIII.'s reign saw no great or general development of accommodation. A large number of houses were built during his reign and that of his predecessor, and it is to this period that may be attributed a great proportion of the domestic work of late Gothic or Tudor character.

Horham Hall, in Essex, is a good example, moderate in size, of this period. It was built in the early years

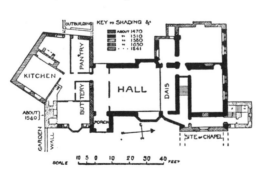

92. Plan of Horham Hall, Essex.

of the sixteenth century by Sir John Cutt, who died in 1520. The plan (Fig. 92) follows the ancient lines, the great hall being in its traditional relationship to the rest of the house. The old indifference to regularity is well illustrated by the passage, treated as a kind of bay window, which leads from the hall to the north wing. The windows in general have but one range of lights, but in the bay of the hall and in the passage, the lingering reluctance to adopt large windows is thrown away (Fig. 93), and we get a foretaste of that vast array of lights which was

93. Horham Hall, Essex (early 16th cent.).

presently to become a distinguishing feature of domestic architecture. There is a large fireplace in the hall and a contemporary louvre in its roof; a somewhat curious combination, inasmuch as the louvre would be needless, either for the escape of smoke or (in view of the large bay window) for the admission of light.

94. Kirtling Hall, Cambridgeshire.
The Gatehouse (early 16th cent.).

There is a strange craving among dwellers in old houses to exaggerate the antiquity of their dwellings. Imagination is fond of peopling with monks halls which were built subsequently to the suppression of the monastic orders, and probably with the wealth acquired in consequence of that event. King John has been made to sleep upon a bed which was constructed when King James was on the throne. A cusped window light will carry its enthusiastic proprietor back two centuries earlier than the facts warrant. But domestic work of a date earlier than Henry VII. is not abundant, and it is probably within the mark to say that nine-tenths of the Gothic stonework of ancient houses and ninety-nine hundredths of the Gothic woodwork are attributable to the time of Henry VII. and Henry VIII.

These new houses were evidently built for pleasure more than for security, although defensive precautions were not entirely omitted. They often occupied the site of an earlier house; but whether this were the case or not, they were generally surrounded by a moat, crossed no longer by a drawbridge, but by one of permanent character. Permanent by comparison, that is to say, for even where moats still remain, bridges of this date are rare; but as a rule the moats have been filled in and the bridges removed, or in any case the moats have been so much filled in as to give easy access to the front entrance.

Some sort of courtyard was contrived in the majority of instances, and as a rule it was surrounded by buildings rather than by a simple wall of defence. The entrance was through a gateway, generally emphasised with a tower over it; indeed one of the characteristic features of large Tudor houses is the lofty tower in which the entrance is set. The bold projecting turrets which usually flank the gateway on each side are a peaceful reminiscence of the defensive towers of earlier times. These gatehouses sometimes rose to a great height. At Oxburgh in Norfolk, Kirtling in Cambridge-shire (Fig. 94), and Cowdray in Sussex, they are from four to six storeys; and the splendid tower at Layer Marney in Essex has as many as eight. The gates were massive, and there was a porter to keep guard, who passed his time in a room adjoining the entrance. In smaller houses where there was no porter there was sometimes a little window or opening commanding a view of the entrance from an adjoining room. It is evident that the household was jealous of strangers, but it was less the bold marauding neighbour whom they feared, than the sturdy beggars who caused no little anxiety to those responsible for the public peace, especially in the years

I

succeeding the suppression of the monasteries, where hitherto mendicants had found shelter and help.

The old reluctance to have large windows in outside walls still lingered ; indeed most of the windows of this period (*i.e.*, the first thirty years of the sixteenth century) are composed of only one row of lights ; the majority of Tudor windows have no transome or cross-bar. In many cases, it is true, the height of the rooms did not call for an upper row of lights. Where, however, there was no reason to restrict window space, particularly in the bay windows of the hall or the principal living rooms, fine lofty windows of many lights were introduced. The bay window and the oriel—by which is here meant a bay window to an upper floor, springing from the wall and not carried down to the ground, of which Kirtling has a fine example (Fig. 94)—were very considerably developed, and may be reckoned among the most striking characteristics of English domestic architecture of this and the Elizabethan periods.

The window heads were still cusped, and, although tracery was very seldom introduced, the upper part was sometimes emphasised by a row of quatrefoils or some similar elaboration (Fig. 91). This obstructing of the top of the window with solid stonework, where the greatest amount of light is to be obtained, was gradually relinquished ; then the simple cusps, which also diminished the light, were dropped, and finally the curved heads gave way to straight ones, and thus the maximum amount of light was secured.

The new fashion in ornament which came in with the Italian influence led to quaint adaptations of ancient features. At Layer Marney, for instance, the cusping is obtained not by bending out a portion of the mullion, a growth springing naturally from its parent stem, but by the introduction of little floriated dolphins " counter-

95. Layer Marney, Essex.

Windows (*cir.* 1520).

The upper range has cusping formed by floriated dolphins, and mullions ornamented with arabesques. The lower range is treated in the customary manner of the Tudor period. There is a row of egg-and-tongue ornament above the cusped corbels over the lower windows.

hauriant "—to use a heraldic term. The mullions, too, are not the splayed or moulded shafts of English tradition, but rectangular shafts with faces elaborately carved with arabesques (Fig. 95). The effect at a distance, where the eye cannot detect the detail, is very like that of a cusped window. So, too, in still later years, where traceried windows were used, as in some of the college halls, the forms of the tracery were ingeniously contrived to accord with the new Italianised detail rather than the old Gothic. At Layer Marney the mixture of the ancient and the modern is further exemplified by the presence of the classic egg-and-tongue ornament above a cusped corbel table, below which are windows with the flat pointed heads characteristic of the Tudor style. At Sutton Place in Surrey, the mixture is again seen. The windows with their pointed and cusped heads are thoroughly Gothic, while the amorini over the door and in the parapet are equally Italian in feeling, though not in delicacy of modelling. The diamond-shaped panels are likewise of southern origin (Fig. 96). Both these houses were built about 1520 to 1525. East Barsham in Norfolk (Fig. 97), which preceded them by about ten years, and resembles them in general style, just misses the Italian detail, although at first sight some of its ornament appears similar to that at Sutton Place. All three houses are of brick with terra-cotta embellishments, and are fine specimens of the brickwork which was used with such excellent effect during the first thirty years of the sixteenth century. A very prevalent custom at this period was to diversify the red brickwork with a diaper of darker bricks.

But, as already said, the new Italian fashion, although it affected the embellishment of the house, was long before it affected the plan. In the reign of Henry VII., indeed, it is nowhere apparent, either in plan or orna-

96. Sutton Place, Surrey.

Part of the Courtyard (1523-25).

ment.   A few prominent dates are useful in fixing on
the mind important changes of style; and the advent
of the Renaissance manner into England can be fixed
by remembering that it made its first appearance in the
tomb of Henry VII. in Westminster Abbey, which was
erected by the order of Henry VIII. in the year 1516.

97. East Barsham, Norfolk.
The Gatehouse (*cir.* 1500-15).

Any work with Italian or Italianised detail, may safely
be dated subsequent to that year.   There is a considerable amount of work of this kind to be found up
and down the country, but chiefly in the southern and
eastern counties.   The only building which it actually

dominated appears to have been Henry VIII.'s house of Nonsuch in Surrey, now entirely destroyed; but in such isolated features as screens, panels, tombs, and doorways, it frequently occurs.

During the reign of Henry VIII., who was a munificent patron of the arts, the new style did much to establish itself, but houses were still arranged on the traditional plan, and were rather haphazard in their disposition. The hall continued to be the principal room; it lay between the family rooms and the servants' quarters. But it was supplemented by retiring rooms of greater size, greater comfort, and greater number. East Barsham (c. 1500-15), Thornbury Castle (c. 1511), Compton Winyates (c. 1520), the enlargement of Lytes Carey manor house (c. 1525), Hengrave Hall (c. 1538), Little Moreton (c. 1559), all these, and others that might be named, show the same free and irregular disposition, which had always been distinctive of the English house.

Hengrave Hall (Fig. 98) is a stepping-stone from the mediæval to the Elizabethan type. It is full of irregularity, but it is planned on much more regular lines than South Wingfield, for instance. The entrance front is symmetrical, although not absolutely so; it has a large central doorway flanked by turrets, and is broken at intervals by other turrets—features quite familiar in sixteenth-century houses. It has a courtyard, encircled on three sides by a corridor, and the hall looks out on to the limited area of the court. The windows are small in comparison with the blank wall spaces, and the detail is Gothic, except for some quasi-Italian amorini supporting the oriel over the front door. While many of the old haphazard arrangements are retained, there is a certain attempt at orderliness and symmetry which points the way to the more regular planning of later years.

Wolsey's great palace at Hampton Court, although planned with considerable attention to symmetry round several rectangular courts, and with an eye to an axial line—arranged, that is to say, with a view to noble and

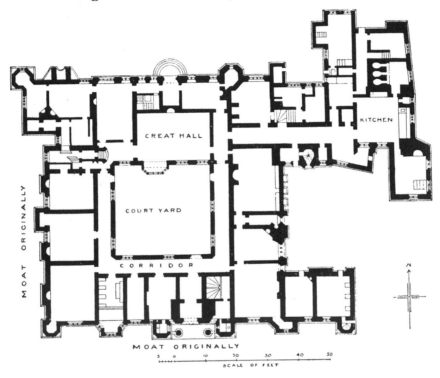

98. Hengrave Hall, Suffolk (*cir.* 1538).
Ground Plan.

dignified effect, was still very irregular both in disposition and in grouping, with roofs of different heights, lofty towers, turrets, and chimneys. Spenser incidentally sketches such palaces in the " Faerie Queene." The house of Pride was " a stately Pallace built of squarèd bricke," where

> " High lifted up were many loftie towres,
>   And goodly galleries far over laid,
>   Full of fair windowes and delightful bowres :
>   And on the top a Diall told the timely howres."

The red-cross knight passing through the gates which
"stood open wide," although in charge of a porter, came
to the hall, "which was on every side with rich array
and costly arras dight." The house of Temperance, too,
was entered through a porch of hewn stone fairly
wrought, provided with a "fayre portcullis" and a gate,
likewise under the charge of a porter, who, unlike the
careless guardian of the house of Pride, duly kept watch
and ward and saw that every one passed in good order
and due regard. The gateway passed, the visitors
came to

> "a stately Hall
> Wherein were many tables fayre dispred."

Thence their hostess led them to see the kitchen,

> "A vaut ybuilt for greate dispense
> With many raunges reard along the wall,
> And one great chimney, whose long tonnell thence
> The smoke forth threw ";

and later,

> "Thence backe againe faire Alma led them right,
> And soone into a goodly Parlour brought
> That was with royal arras richly dight."

The only other part of her house to which Alma took
her guests was a turret,

> "Therein were divers rowmes and divers stages,
> But three the chiefest and of greatest powre."

No other rooms are particularly mentioned, but these
glimpses at the palaces of Spenser's days bring before
our vision their gatehouses, their towers and turrets, their
long galleries, and their many windows. It is both
interesting and curious to find that even to Spenser, who
wrote in the latter part of the sixteenth century (the
"Faerie Queene" was being written in 1580), the hall,
the kitchen, and the parlour were still the principal

apartments. Except for the sumptuous hangings and the other embellishments with which he adorns his rooms, and except for the parlour and gallery, the houses which he pictures resemble those of Chaucer. The parlour, however, stands for a good deal ; it typifies the extension which had taken place in the family apartments. Spenser's descriptions, too, although indicating no great advance in the classification of rooms, point to a much more magnificent furnishing and adornment than anything to be found in Chaucer's.

During Spenser's life, however, a very great advance was being made in domestic architecture, and in particular the planning of houses was receiving especial attention, and was being undertaken by trained experts. Doubtless the growth of Italian ideas had something to do with this. Symmetry of disposition, instead of being occasionally adopted, had become universal, and it required more than the skill of a home-bred mason, such as hitherto had devised houses, to arrange the increased accommodation now necessary, within the requisite symmetrical outline, and at the same time to ensure a workable relation of rooms one to the other. In addition to this a considerable acquaintance with the new fashion in detail was required of designers, and accordingly not a few of them made tours abroad to France and even as far as Italy in order to familiarise themselves with foreign methods and to bring to their work the most novel ideas of the time.

CHAPTER VIII.

LATE SIXTEENTH CENTURY—SYMMETRY IN PLANNING.

THE best known of the designers of this period is John Thorpe, who lived in the reigns of Elizabeth and James ; and his collection of drawings, preserved in the Soane Museum, is of great value from the light it throws on the house design of the time. Houses themselves have generally undergone many alterations, from which it is difficult to disentangle their history, or to tell with certainty what their original plan may have been. But Thorpe's drawings show what the designer actually had in his mind as he worked. From them we learn that in most cases the hall was still the chief apartment, and that it still occupied its ancient situation between the family rooms on one side and the servants' rooms on the other. In the great majority of examples the daïs is also shown, indicating that the ancient usage was maintained of the family occupying the head of the hall at meals, while the servants were ranged at tables in the body. But we know from other sources that some families had already taken to dining in a separate room, and that guests had complained of being set to dine with the steward in the hall instead of with the family in the parlour. On some of Thorpe's plans a "dining parlour" is provided ; on many of them there is a "winter parlour," placed within easy distance of the kitchen. There is also an instance of a "servants' dining-room," and of a "hall for hynds." These all tend to show that the hall was losing its old importance as the centre of life in the house. Such a fate was only natural considering by how many other rooms it was now supplemented. There were the "great chamber," the "withdrawing-room," and the "long gallery" among the larger rooms; the "parlour," the "breakfast-room," and the "study" among the smaller. In addition to these, which were day rooms, were many "bed-chambers" and "lodgings," which were in fact bedrooms. The accommodation for the family and guests was therefore as complete as could be desired—as complete, in fact, as at the present day, if we except the very important item of bath-rooms and other sanitary conveniences. The drawback is that the rooms, although far more skilfully planned than of old, were subject to an almost rigidly symmetrical outline, preventing that compactness which is now aimed at; and as the various wings of the house were as a rule only one room wide, it followed that some of the rooms had to be thoroughfare rooms. This arrangement cannot have been held to be vastly inconvenient in those days, nor for many days to come, for it continued until well into the eighteenth century.

The subdivision in the servants' quarters was as ample as in those of the family. The "kitchen" was still, as it always had been, the principal room on this side. The "buttery" and the "pantry" were also of long standing. But the "pastry" had come in almost every instance to supplement the kitchen, being the place where the baking was done, and being furnished almost invariably with two ovens. The "dry larder" and "wet larder" were equally frequent, and so was the "survaying place," or serving-room. There are also to be found in the larger houses a "scullery," a "meal house," "bolting-house," "spicery," "trencher," "pewter," and "brush." The steward, his clerk, the butler, the pantler, and the waiters are all found to have their own separate rooms. How widely different is all this from the ancient custom of the whole household living by day and night in the great hall !

The need for the great hall, indeed, was passing away. Already in a few of Thorpe's plans it is found to be arranged in a manner no longer suitable for its old purposes. In some it is placed out of its central position. By the end of the first quarter of the seventeenth century it had practically lost its ancient character of the chief living room, and had become little more than a fine vestibule leading to the actual living rooms and the rest of the house.

Reproductions of a few of Thorpe's drawings will serve to illustrate the Elizabethan and Jacobean type of plan even better than plans of actual houses. They link themselves at one end to the mediæval type, and they lead at the other to that altered treatment of the hall which marks the definite break with mediævalism. It is unfortunate that there is no means of fixing their various dates ; the sequence in which they are placed is therefore not necessarily chronological. They represent types of arrangement of which many other instances may be found in Thorpe's collection. First, there is the courtyard plan (Fig. 99), the modernised version of the defensive court of earlier times. Here all thought of defence is abandoned, save that the main entrance is through an archway overlooked by the porter. Visitors are not repelled by frowning gateways, a grim portcullis, and blind walls pierced with nothing but hostile slits. On the contrary, access is made easy and inviting. A flight of steps leads on to a terrace, and thence direct to the main door ; cheerful windows fill the walls, arranged not only to give light within and a view without, but also to enliven the structure itself with the ordered rhythm of

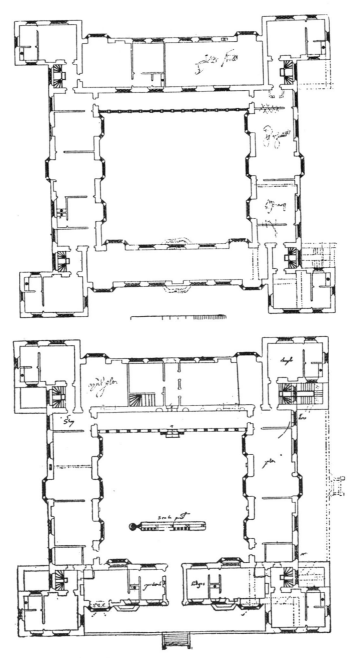

99. Ground and Upper Plans of an Unnamed House.

From the Thorpe Collection.

their glittering panes. The courtyard is handsomely furnished with stately bays running the full height of the walls ; a long range of arches faces the entrance, and forms a loggia beneath which is the door to the screens. The external facades are designed with equal care. At each corner there is a massive pavilion, and from one to the other stretch the main walls sparkling with windows, which are relieved from monotony by the introduction of further bays.

There is no haphazard planning about this house ; everything is carefully thought out ; the effect of every projection, every window, and every chimney is considered. Yet with all this symmetry and formality, the underlying arrangement follows the old lines. The hall is entered through the screens ; it has its daïs, its bay, and its fireplace near to its upper end ; from this end are approached the family rooms—the parlour, the chapel, and the principal stairs, leading to the great chamber, the withdrawing-room, and the long gallery. On the other side of the house, but downstairs, lie the kitchens in the basement.

The next plan (Fig. 100) is that of a house with a fore-court, only (as explained on the drawing itself) the court, with its diagonally placed entrance lodges, should have been drawn on the front of the house instead of being detached and at the back. But this correction made—and it will be easier done by looking at Kip's view (Fig. 101)—it will be seen that a reminiscence of the old jealousy of approach is still found in the walled court and its entrance lodges; otherwise the house is obviously built without a thought of protection. It is contrived for display combined with convenience. Its terraces and long symmetrical fronts are the means towards the first, while the second is greatly helped by the passage, or "longe entry throughe all," which runs the whole length

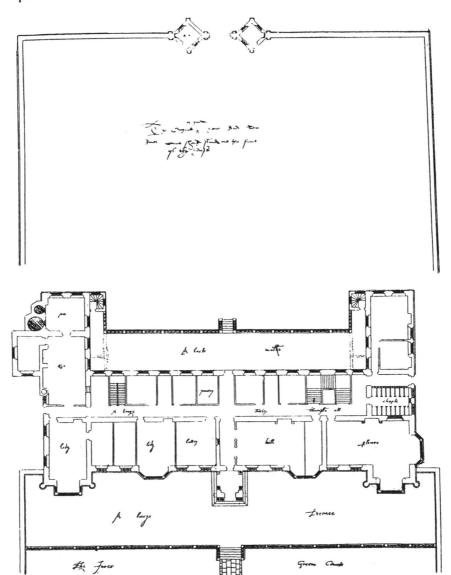

100. Ground Plan (unnamed).

From the Thorpe Collection.

It is probably Beaufort House, Chelsea.

of the house. This is a feature quite new in house planning, so far. Otherwise the ancient dispositions are adopted; the hall lies to the right of the screens, and beyond it the parlour and chapel; to the left the buttery,

pantry, and (at some distance) the kitchen. Kip's view
shows the dignified but simple treatment of the exterior,
and the surrounding courts and gardens. The plan is
not named in Thorpe's drawing, but it agrees so closely

101. Beaufort House, Chelsea, Kip's View.

with Kip's view as to leave little doubt that it is the
same house—namely, Beaufort House in Chelsea, built
by Robert Cecil, Earl of Salisbury, during the closing
years of the sixteenth century, by way either of enlarging

K

or replacing an earlier house, which had been the home of Sir Thomas More.

The next plan is of the **H** type, which was widely employed at this period (Fig. 102). Without entering into minute detail it will suffice to draw attention to the maintenance of the time-honoured position of the hall between the family rooms and the servants' quarters ; to the provision of a winter parlour near the kitchen; to the

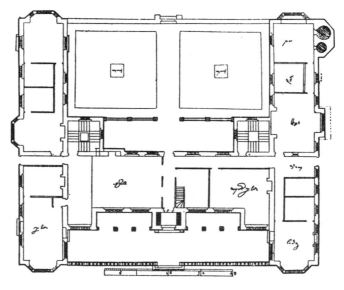

102. Ground Plan (unnamed).

From the Thorpe Collection.

strict symmetry of the general plan, and to the many windows, arranged not only to give light to the rooms, but also by their ordered disposition to impart a distinctive character to the appearance of the building. To such an extent is this symmetrical treatment carried, that in the "lodging" near the winter parlour, two of the windows are crippled by the fireplace, with the result that they become in part shams. This is a striking testimony to the change which was coming

over house design.   Hitherto windows had been provided for the sake of light within ; now they are
regarded as means of obtaining effect without.   The
other characteristic features to be observed are the
balustraded terraces on the front and back ; the arcades
on either side of the porch ; and the court at the back
with a fountain placed on each side of the central paved
walk.   There is no elevation corresponding to this plan,

103. Old Somerset House, in the Strand.   (Now demolished.)

End façade of Courtyard.

but the general effect of the front may be gathered from
a view of old Somerset House in the Strand, although
this is on a rather more important scale (Fig. 103).   Here
also is a central porch flanked by arcades which stop
against square projecting windows in the corner of the
courtyard.

   The last of the series (Fig. 104) shows the beginning
of a change in the hall.   The screen is no longer a

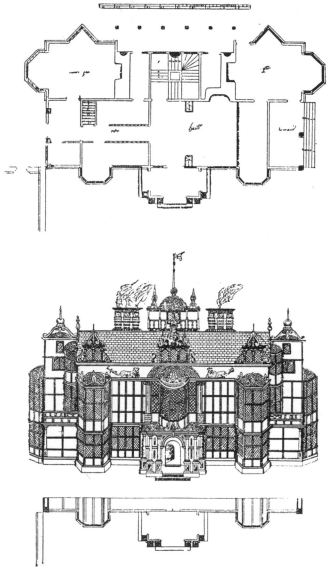

104. Elevation and Plan of a House (unnamed).

From the Thorpe Collection.

continuous partition cutting off a passage.   It has shrunk
to something that is a mere projection from the side
walls, affording no shelter from the cross-traffic of the
front door.   Indeed the front door, which formerly had

been the common entrance for the whole household, was gradually being reserved for the family and the guests, the servants being provided with a separate entrance of their own. The elevation is an interesting specimen of Elizabethan design in half-timber.

The arrangement of the hall shown in this example greatly detracts from its comfort as a living room, in spite of the fact that the retention of the daïs (indicated by the hatched line across the hall) points to its use as such. It is a first step in the direction of using the hall as a vestibule and not as a room. A more striking instance of this change is to be found at Aston Hall near Birmingham (finished in 1635). Thorpe's plan of it shows the great hall following the ancient lines with the entrance at one end into the screens. But when built the front door was placed centrally at once with the façade and the hall. This new position, delivering the traffic into its centre, wholly precluded the use of the hall as a living room ; it became in fact a vestibule. With this change the link with mediævalism was severed. It marks in a striking manner the parting of the ways ; the change from the old to the new ; the closing of the long chapter of domestic planning which began in the early days of the twelfth century ; the final abandonment of the principle which had dominated house planning for five hundred years.

Overlapping Thorpe in point of date, but out-living him by a good many years—so far as the uncertainty surrounding the lives of such simple persons enables us to judge—was the John Smithson whose drawings * have been preserved with as much care as those of Thorpe. He died in 1634, and was buried at Bolsover :

---

* They are in the possession of Colonel Coke of Brookhill Hall, Alfreton. See also pp. 183, 185.

he left a son, Huntingdon Smithson, who also was an architectural designer. The Smithson collection rivals the other in interest. It does not afford quite so vivid an insight into the methods of the house planner; but it contains a greater variety of subjects. It shows equally clearly the change which was taking place in the disposition of the chief rooms: how the hall was being deposed from its pre-eminence; and how corridors were becoming more frequent. The principal apartments include no new names: they consist still of the hall, the parlour, the great chamber, the withdrawing-room, the chapel, and the long gallery. The houses still have terraces and arcades, and are still flanked by courts. The courtyard type and the H type are the most prevalent. The elevations are less full of fancy than those of Elizabeth's time; the detail is more ponderous and may even be regarded as clumsy. There are many features—doors, windows, gateways—described as "Italyan," showing how the demand was increasing for detail which was more strictly Italian in character than anything that had hitherto been produced. Thorpe, it must be remembered, was in the heyday of his career in Elizabeth's time; Smithson in James I.'s. The earliest date connected with Thorpe is 1570, in which year he tells us he laid the first stone of Kirby in Northamptonshire. The latest date on the Smithson drawings is 1632. The two collections afford an admirable panorama of house-building during a period of sixty years—a period which saw architecture free itself from the slackening grasp of mediævalism; which witnessed the new birth of Science, and beheld Poetry gain the sublime heights to which Shakespeare led it, and whither it has never quite succeeded in ascending again.

During this remarkable period were built some of

105. Montacute House, Somerset (1580).

The two-storey screen between the wings is of earlier date (*cir.* 1520) and was brought from Clifton Maybank.

the largest houses which England ever possessed. Holdenby (1580), so far as the house itself went, was larger than the great palaces of Blenheim and Castle Howard. Its fronts were 360 ft. and 224 ft. long, as against 320 ft. and 220 ft. at Blenheim, and 324 ft. and 210 ft. at Castle Howard. But in both the later houses there were subsidiary courts attached which greatly lengthened the total extent. Audley End (1610) covered even more ground than Holdenby, its frontages extending to 470 ft. and 280 ft.: but more than half its area was occupied by a subsidiary court, whereas almost the whole of Holdenby consisted of important rooms. But rivalry in dimensions apart, it must be remembered that the designer of Holdenby had no precedent to look to, no great house to outvie. Hampton Court excepted, his was the first mansion, built for pleasure and for state, which had been conceived on so large a scale. There were also many other houses which, though smaller, were of the first importance. Such were Buckhurst House in Sussex ; Burghley House and Kirby Hall both, like Holdenby, in Northamptonshire ; Theobalds in Hertfordshire ; Knole in Kent. The reason for erecting these large houses, or at any rate for making them so extensive, was stated by at least two of their builders. Lord Burghley and Sir Christopher Hatton both said that it was in order to accommodate the Queen that they were led to so much extravagance.

But the building fever seems to have been in the air. Almost every nobleman and squire in the country either rebuilt, enlarged, or altered his house. Sheldons manor house in Wiltshire is a charming example of alteration (see Frontispiece). The original house, of which the porch is a part, was built by the Gascelyns in the fourteenth century. The sixteenth-century addition with its rectangular, mullioned windows, was built over earlier walls by the Hungerfords, and to their successors may be attributed the eighteenth-century gate piers. Like many old manor houses, Sheldons has ceased to be the home of the squire, and has become a farmhouse. In half the villages of England there is either a house of the Elizabethan period or the memory of one. Not only did the landed gentry build, but also rich merchants in

106. Lyveden Old Building, Northamptonshire.

(Early 17th cent.)

London and many of the provincial towns. A vast number of these houses have been swept away, but happily a great many still remain of all degrees of importance, from great seats like Montacute in Somerset (Fig. 105), or Burton Agnes in Yorkshire, down to the unpretending manor houses to be found among the steep declivities of the Cotswolds or the gentler undulations of Northamptonshire (Fig. 106). A proof (were it wanted) of the disappearance of many fine houses of this time is to be found in the Thorpe and Smithson drawings, for it is but a small proportion of the houses there shown that is known to be still in existence.

CHAPTER IX.

Elizabethan and Jacobean Houses—Exteriors.

THE characteristic feature of Elizabethan and Jacobean houses is the square-headed mullioned windows (see Fig. 110). Previous to the time of Elizabeth, the plain square head hardly ever occurs; it is always pointed. Down to the end of the fifteenth century it was usually cusped (see Fig. 66). In the early part of the sixteenth century, that is, in Tudor houses, it became flat pointed and the cuspings disappeared. This form lingered on until it was superseded by the square head. It may, however, be found in a few instances as late as the second decade in the seventeenth century, but the cases are not many.

The use of the bay window was greatly developed in Elizabethan and Jacobean times. It was, as already stated, frequently utilised as one of the most important architectural features of a façade. This may be observed on some of Thorpe's plans (Figs. 99, 100, 104), in Kip's view of Longleat (Fig. 107), as well as in nearly all the illustrations given of the houses of this period (see Figs. 116, 119, 124, 125, 126). Besides the simple and dignified forms which were chiefly used, there were a few cases in which the plan was more complicated, and in which it took one shape on the ground floor and another on the floor above. Thorpe has several instances of this quaint treatment; an actual example exists at Thornbury Castle (Fig. 108) where the result is not very happy. A more successful attempt was made at Sir Paul Pindar's house

107. Longleat House, Wiltshire (*cir.* 1550-80), Kip's View.

in Bishopsgate Street, now in the Victoria and Albert Museum (Fig. 109). Here the different planes of the straight lights combined with the circular projection in the middle, the busy pattern of the glazing, and the carved panels, produce an extremely rich effect.

Another characteristic of the Elizabethan house is the employment of the classic cornice. In Gothic buildings the horizontal "string-course," or projecting moulding of stone, was very frequently used. It served to bind the design together and to give it unity and coherence. It was usually of small depth and slight projection. But with the in-

108. Bay Window at Thornbury Castle, Gloucestershire.

109. Window from Sir Paul Pindar's House, Bishopsgate.
Now in the Victoria and Albert Museum.

vasion of Italian fashions, came the Italian profiles of
stonework, and the string-courses of the old days were
replaced by cornices, more elaborate in section, of greater
depth and greater projection. The old thin string-

110. Kirby Hall, Northamptonshire.

A Corner of the Courtyard (1575).

courses were not entirely abandoned, but they received a slightly different section, more in harmony than the old forms with the new classic profiles.   Pilasters were

111. Tudor Chimneys from Aston Bury, Herts.

also introduced with the cornices, and some of the grander buildings were adorned with several of the "orders" placed one over the other.   In time it became "correct" to use the Doric order on the first storey, the

Ionic on the second, and the Corinthian on the third. These pilasters were generally of no practical use : they were merely ornamental features, and were sometimes carried up not with a view to supporting a crowning cornice, but to finish with a finial—a heraldic animal or what-not— altogether out of scale with what it stood on. Such pilasters and cornices were never employed previous to the reign of Henry VIII., and did not come into general use until the time of Elizabeth. The courtyard at Kirby Hall is furnished with them (Fig. 110) ; nevertheless, however wrong they may be judged from the academic stand - point, it cannot be denied that they materially help the composition, and combine with the many lights of the mullioned windows to produce a picturesque and romantic effect.

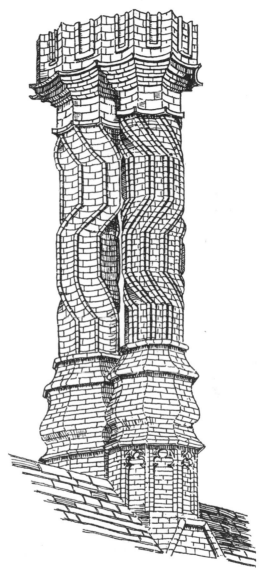

112. Tudor Chimneys from Droit-wich, Worcestershire.

(Now destroyed.)

The chimneys of Elizabethan houses are far simpler than those of Tudor times. It was in the reign of Henry

VIII. that chimneys assumed their most elaborate forms, whether in stone or brick. They were twisted, counter-twisted, minutely panelled, or surrounded by spiral bands of various profiles (Figs. 111, 112), with a profusion of complication that must have taxed the skill of the craftsman of the time, as it certainly does the skill of the draughtsman of to-day. But with the more "regular" feeling which came with Italian detail, this excessive play of fancy died out, and chimneys became simpler in their design, often consisting merely of straight shafts standing on a good base and covered with an ample cap

113. Pilton Manor House, Northamptonshire. (Now the Rectory.)

(Fig. 106). Sometimes this plain form was Italianised into a complete column with its appropriate base and cap, and crowned with a short length of the corresponding classic entablature. But whatever form their detail may have taken, the designers of the time ordinarily used the mass of their chimneys as an important architectural feature. They grouped two or three fireplaces together, carried up a great stack of stone or brickwork, and placed their flues in single shafts upon it, thus combining solidity below with a pleasing lightness against the sky.

In the larger houses these various features—mullioned windows, cornices, pilasters, and chimneys—were used with a lavish hand. The mullioned windows of many lights were framed in pilasters furnished with their appropriate pedestals, bases, and caps ; at every floor level a great entablature with architrave, ornamental frieze, and far projecting cornice made the circuit of the building : above all rose the gables, often straight of outline, but not infrequently fashioned into graceful

114. Sydenham House Devonshire (*cir.* 1600).

curves ; from gable to gable extended a balustraded parapet ; at due intervals along the walls projected great chimney-stacks carrying slender shafts separated from each other by narrow spaces of daylight. The whole was a serious and determined effort at design, widely different from the simple and often fortuitous arrangement of a mediæval house, where the various parts, beautiful though they were in themselves, were not co-ordinated in the same resolute manner.

In the smaller houses effort was not so conspicuous. The designers drew upon the same sources for their effects—mullioned windows, classic string-courses, steep gables, and fine chimney-stacks—but they were more modest in their use of them, and refrained from employing pilasters, except perhaps to a doorway. Between the simplicity of the small manor house and the magnificence of the nobleman's mansion lay every degree of elaboration, and a series of examples might be brought together

115. Moyns Park, Essex.

forming a continuous *crescendo* from a squire's home like Pilton Manor house in Northamptonshire (Fig. 113), through such houses as Sydenham in Devonshire (Fig. 114), or Moyns Park in Essex (Fig. 115), up to splendid mansions like the home of the younger branch of the Cecils at Hatfield (Fig. 116).

Moyns Park has a special interest, inasmuch as it is one of the fairly numerous cases in which a house of the first half of the sixteenth century was superseded by a

116. Hatfield House, the North Front (1611).

117. Derwent Hall, Derbyshire.

finer one in the second half. Here the low, gabled, half-timber building is of the earlier date, and the lofty one, with its row of fine brick chimneys, is of the later. There could hardly have been forty years between the two buildings; the earlier has some excellent detail, especially on the long front not shown in the illustration: it was a fine house of its kind; and yet such was the passion for new houses that it was soon superseded by its loftier and more monumental neighbour.

The general appearance of houses of this time may be gathered from the illustrations, which comprise examples from various districts of England, and serve to show, among other things, that the same treatment was adopted over the whole country, varied according to local circumstances. Where stone was abundant, the houses were of stone, with more or less elaborate detail according to the hardness of the material. On the great beds of easily worked Oolite which stretch from Somerset and Wiltshire through Oxfordshire, Gloucestershire and Northamptonshire into Lincolnshire, the work is often both rich and delicate, and has acquired through time and weather a soft grey tint enlivened by the partial incrustation of many-hued lichens. In Derbyshire, Yorkshire, and Lancashire where the stone is much harder, the work is of a plainer and more severe type, such as may be seen at Derwent Hall (Fig. 117), and the colour is more sombre. In the eastern counties brick is frequently the chief material, with stone where wrought detail is required, such as quoins, cornices, parapets, and pilasters. Felbrigge Hall in Norfolk (Fig. 118), probably built by Thomas Windham, who died in 1653 at the age of eighty-two, is a good example. In some instances where stone was not easily to be had, the detail which would otherwise have been in that material, was worked in plaster to imitate it.

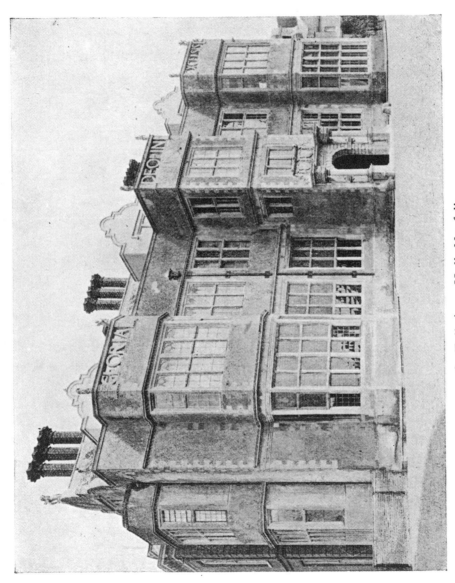

118. Felbrigge Hall, Norfolk.
(Early 17th cent.)

In the western counties timber and plaster were freely used ; Cheshire, Lancashire, Worcestershire, and Herefordshire afford the finest and most ornamental examples of this method of construction,⸱while Kent, Surrey, and Sussex in the south have a fair amount of plainer work of the same kind.   In these houses the main walls are formed of stout timber framed together, with the interstices filled in with lath and plaster.   The structural timbers are left visible ; most of them are

119. Marton Hall, Cheshire.   (Now destroyed.)

vertical, but they are braced together at intervals by horizontal timbers, and are occasionally further strengthened by sloping struts.   This framework itself makes a pleasing pattern and satisfies the eye as to the strength and stability of the fabric.   The timbers are always of large scantling, and are nearly equal in their total area to the spaces that are left between them. These characteristics are common to all the examples illustrated (Figs. 119-123).   But whereas in the southern counties, and to a great extent in Worcestershire, the

120. Bramhall Hall, near Stockport, Cheshire.

designers were satisfied to leave their work in this simple form, in Lancashire, and more particularly in Cheshire, they added interest and richness to the effect by placing curved braces within some of the panels, thus producing patterns of more or less intricacy. Variations in the shape of the curves resulted in variations of pattern, and the variety of effects thus obtained

121. Shell Farm, near Droitwich, Worcestershire.

is quite remarkable. A simple example is Marton Hall, near Congleton, now destroyed (Fig. 119); a more elaborate one is the well-known Little Moreton Hall in the same district. But the finest specimen of a half-timber house is Bramhall Hall, near Stockport (Fig. 120), which is not only quaint and picturesque, but in places approaches as near to stateliness as such homely

materials allow.   Lancashire at one time fell little short
of Cheshire in attractive examples, but before the
constant spread of its manufacturing centres they are
rapidly disappearing.   Throughout large districts of
Worcestershire such black-and-white houses as that
at Shell Farm (Fig. 121) may be seen.   They are

122. The Manor House, Sedlescombe, Sussex.

quite simple, but they give a cheerful aspect to the
countryside, especially when the spring time surrounds
them with bright green foliage and the pink and white
blossoms of the orchards.   In Sussex and Kent the use
of half-timber work was not so general, nor was there
nearly as much play of fancy as in Cheshire, the design

being seldom of more elaborate character than that at Sedlescombe (Fig. 122) and Brad Street (Fig. 123).

In Kent, Surrey, and Sussex, too, occurs in its perfection the quaint and picturesque custom of hanging external walls with tiles, the relative softness of which is favourable to the growth of lichens, and results in those brilliant bits of colour so dear to the water-colour sketcher. Every district has its own character, and the

123. House at Brad Street, Kent.

wise man will enjoy each in turn; no more expecting to find the brilliance of Surrey among the greys of Northamptonshire, than lamenting the absence of the soft tones of the Midlands among the wild moorlands of the North.

One great charm of the houses of this period is their marvellous variety of treatment, although nearly always subject to a symmetrical arrangement and a general similarity of plan. A central porch between projecting wings of greater or less length is almost universal, although there are not a few instances of square houses,

124. Heath Hall, near Wakefield Yorkshire
(Early 17th cent.)

such as Felbrigge (Fig. 118) or Heath Hall (Fig. 124). The windows, too, are practically always composed of

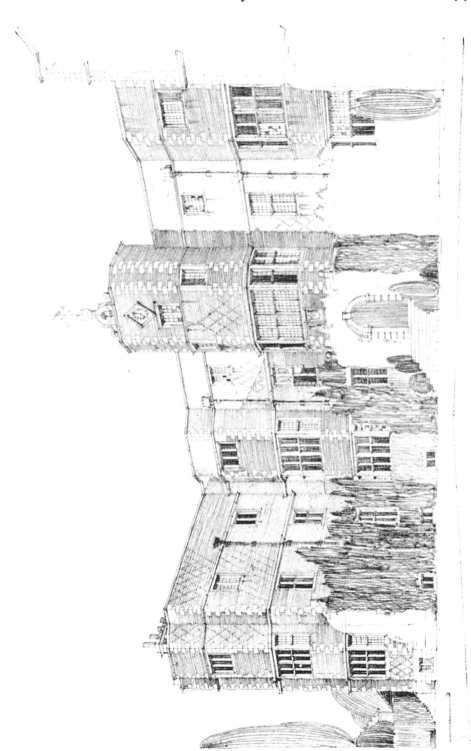

125. Quenby Hall, Leicestershire (*cir.* 1620).

126. Gayhurst, Buckinghamshire (1597 and later).

numerous rectangular lights. But some houses had turrets; some had gables either straight or curved; some had flat lead-covered roofs as at Longleat, Quenby in Leicestershire (Fig. 125), or Temple Newsam in Yorkshire; and some combine both treatments, as at Gayhurst in Buckinghamshire (Fig. 126). This house is said to have been built by a Mulsho in 1597, and to have been much improved a few years afterwards by William Mulsho. This double period of building may, perhaps, account for the combination of the flat roofs and the gables. It subsequently passed by marriage to Everard Digby, and is one of the innumerable places where, tradition says, the Gunpowder Plot was hatched. There was a marked desire for a picturesque sky-line, which led, in some flat-roofed houses like Heath Hall, Barlborough in Derbyshire, and Hatfield House (Fig. 116), to the carrying up of bay windows to form turrets above the parapet. Chimneys were most frequently taken up in separate flues, but occasionally in solid stacks. Parapets were sometimes solid as at Gayhurst and Quenby; more frequently balustraded as at Longleat, and occasionally formed of stone letters making a sentence. Felbrigge Hall has a short one, "Gloria Deo in excelsis"; Temple Newsam in Yorkshire and Castle Ashby in Northamptonshire bear long sentences which make almost the complete circuit of the roofs.

Every house of any importance was surrounded with some kind of lay-out. The external courtyard, which originated from a desire for protection, was converted into a place of pleasure or state, yet still retaining the advantage of preventing unrestricted access. Small manor houses, such as that at Cold Ashton in Somerset, or Eyam Hall in Derbyshire, had at least a walled garden in front with a terrace approached up a flight of steps. Large houses had several courts in front, which

had each to be traversed in turn before the front door
was reached, as well as side courts and walled gardens.
Many of them had a small entrance archway in the wall
of the courtyard, generally of simple design, but imparting a touch of interest and romance to an otherwise

127. Entrance Gateway at West Burton, Sussex.

unpretentious home, as is the case at West Burton in
Sussex (Fig. 127). Nearly all these characteristic adjuncts have now been cleared away from our English
houses, to their grievous detriment; and it has been
remarked that had we but retained the shelter of our

128. Brome Hall, Suffolk (*cir.* 1580).

ancient garden walls, we should be under much less necessity to seek the warmth of the Riviera during the cold winds of spring. No better idea of the ancient aspect of Jacobean houses can be gained than from the views of Knyff and Kip; and although the accuracy of every detail cannot be guaranteed, there can be no doubt that the general disposition is fairly true to the facts. At Brome Hall in Suffolk (Fig. 128) the approach to the entrance front is across at least two courts, and if the outermost enclosure is anything more than the end of an avenue, there would be three. The other fronts are surrounded with walled gardens which extend a considerable distance on every side, and are backed up by plantations and a wide avenue. The house itself is plain in character, depending for its effect largely upon its symmetrical arrangement. There is a certain amount of richness about the porch and the tower over it; elsewhere the prominent chimney-stacks and the dormer windows are the dominating features. It will be observed that the sides of the first garden court (beyond the avenue) are formed of subsidiary buildings, the range on the left being one side of the stable court. It was quite customary to give architectural importance to the principal approach by means of inferior buildings, which in the present day are kept out of observation. At Longleat (Fig. 107) the lay-out is confined to three sides of the house; the approach lies along a raised paved walk. The "regular" and symmetrical fronts, which here also depend upon bay windows for their interest, enclose buildings which are less severely treated and which blossom out into many turrets. Much of this inside work is of somewhat earlier date, for Longleat was the result of several different building efforts which extended over a period of about thirty years, and concluded about 1580. In these descriptions it is Kip's

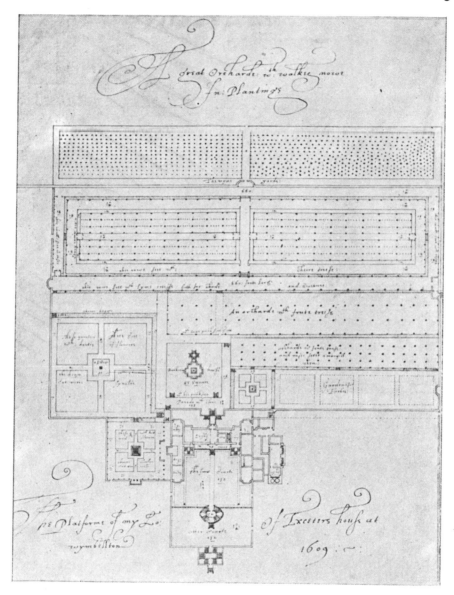

129. Plan of the Lay-out of Lord Exeter's House and Garden
at Wimbledon, 1609.

From the Smithson Collection.

views which are referred to, not the present buildings,
which have in most cases undergone alterations, especially in respect of their lay-outs.

The grand period of garden design was to come later, in the early years of the eighteenth century, at the time when Knyff and Kip published their book.   But if proof

130. Powis Castle, Wales.

were wanted that the later draughtsman did not invent the elaborate surroundings of his houses, it is to be found among the Smithson drawings which were made in the first quarter of the seventeenth century. There are several plans of lay-outs in the collection, the most notable being the survey of Wimbledon House, made in 1609 (Fig. 129). This was a Cecil house, having been built in the year 1588 by either Lord Burghley or his son, afterwards Earl of Exeter. It stood on the edge of a high hill with a splendid prospect towards the north. The steepness of the ground on this side led to the formation of two courts, approached by fine flights of steps, and leading to a terrace off which the front door opened. Behind the house, to the south, lay the great garden, and on the east was a small sunk garden, called in later years the Orange garden. Smithson's notes indicate the principal features : a banqueting house, hedges of thorn and quick-set cut very finely, quarters set with knots of flowers, rows of cherry trees, rows of lime trees, " both for shade and sweetness," and various orchards. Here again we have striking evidence of how far we have travelled from the enclosures which surrounded the castles of two centuries earlier, even the largest, such as Kenilworth.

Everything, indeed, points to the new delight which people were taking in their homes ; how they loved not only fine houses but fine gardens, seizing upon every change of level to introduce a terrace, and charmed with any opportunity to form a handsome flight of steps, such as that at Heath Hall (Fig. 124), or Powis Castle in Wales (Fig. 130). It is quite clear that the days were past when men merely ornamented what was essential to safety : they now revelled in their freedom from restriction, and indulged themselves in attractive design for its own sake.

CHAPTER X.

ELIZABETHAN AND JACOBEAN HOUSES—INTERIORS.

THE same impulse which brought about so great a change in external treatment, led also to corresponding developments in the internal decorations: magnificence and comfort went hand in hand. The great chimneys which have been referred to as forming such conspicuous features outside, implied a considerable increase of fire-places within. Harrison, in his contribution to "Hollin-shed's Chronicles" (1577), mentions "the multitude of chimneys lately erected." Every room of importance by this time had at least one, and the large rooms frequently had two. It was this multiplication of flues which led to their striking external treatment. The increase was only one of the effects of the continual pursuit of comfort which underlay all the changes in domestic arrangement. In other directions the pursuit was successful owing to the changed condition of the times, which no longer demanded security against attack. Elizabethan houses were built for comfort, and many of them for magnificence. Being no longer hampered by the need for precautions against forcible entry, designers laid themselves out to obtain a convenient disposition of rooms so far as that was compatible with a dignified, and often splendid, treatment, and the demands of a symmetry which grew more and more insistent. The accommodation of the larger houses of that time suffices for the present day, although its disposition is often at variance with our wants. The actual decoration of the rooms is still frequently taken as a model for imitation and even reproduction.

The bare walls of mediæval houses had already been plastered in the better rooms, and the plaster had been ornamented in various simple ways by painted patterns. This custom was still retained to a certain extent in Elizabeth's time.   But the old fashion of wainscoting rooms, that is, panelling with oak, was considerably extended, and all the principal rooms were thus treated. The development of panelling is of much interest, but is of rather too intricate a nature to be traced here in any detail: suffice it to say that the earliest form of ornamental panels appears to be what is called the linen pattern, in which the surface of the panel itself was so carved as to bear a resemblance to a piece of stiffly and symmetrically folded linen (Fig. 131).   This fashion was in vogue from the latter part of the fifteenth century, throughout the reign of Henry VII. and well into that of Henry VIII. With the advent of the Italian manner, the panels became carved with large and somewhat coarse arabesque work, fantastic animals were intro-

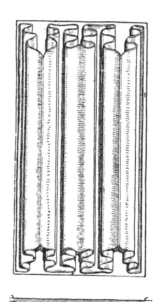

131. A Linen Panel.

duced, and, notably, human heads set in circular frames (Fig. 132).   Another pattern peculiar to this period, and one which can neither trace a certain origin from anything before it, nor be traced through any direct descendant, is partly shown in the same illustration.   It is formed of two curved ribs set back to back, but in this particular instance the circular panel is interposed between the upper and lower halves of the pattern. A panel from Layer Marney (Fig. 133) shows it more clearly, and it is just possible that in the panel at South Kensington (Fig. 134) we have the origin of this curious and fleeting

132. Wood Panelling at the Bishop's Palace, Norwich
(*temp*. Henry VIII.).

form.   Elizabethan panelling is less fanciful in treatment, its effect being obtained, when anything more elaborate than oblong moulded panels was introduced, not by carving, but an increased intricacy of framing, and occasionally by an inlay of coloured wood. This intricacy became more pronounced in Jacobean work, which on the whole is more complicated than Elizabethan. A fine example of early seventeenth-century panelling

133. Panel at Layer Marney, 134. Wood Panel in the Victoria
Essex.   and Albert Museum.

is to be seen at Calgarth Old Hall in Westmorland (Fig. 135), where the main panels are subdivided by an insertion of diamond shape, and the topmost tier is in every case arched. An invariable characteristic of panelling down to about 1630 is the comparatively small size of the panels, which seldom exceeded 2 ft. in their longest dimension. They offer in this respect a complete

135. Calgarth Old Hall, Westmorland.
(Early 17th cent.)

contrast to those which came into vogue about the middle of the seventeenth century. But, although the great amount of panelling which still survives in all parts of the country shows that it was universally adopted, yet the old-fashioned tapestry played an important part in the clothing of the walls, from the splendid pieces, brought from all parts of Europe, with which Cardinal Wolsey adorned his great palace of Hampton Court, down to the "smirched worm-eaten tapestry" of Borachio's illustration, or the arras of the inn where Falstaff soaked himself in such an intolerable deal of sack.

The plasterer's art blossomed out into wonderful results. Founding his designs at first on the wood-ribbed ceilings of his youth, he gradually elaborated them into the amazing richness which characterises the end of the sixteenth century. The variety of his patterns is wonderful, and, considering the number of ceilings which are left, it is surprising how seldom two instances of the same design are found. As a rule great judgment was shown in the choice of patterns : simple designs of slight projection being used in low rooms, and more elaborate ones of heavier section in lofty rooms. Frequently in the latter the principal points in the design were emphasised by pendants, which broke the monotony and added greatly to the richness of the effect.

At Parham in Sussex (Fig. 136) is an example of this treatment, which, indeed, would be almost meagre, were it not for the pendants. This room is the great hall, and, it will be observed, is covered with a flat ceiling instead of an open timber roof. The latter form of covering, which had been customary from the earliest times, was giving place, in the early part of the seventeenth century, to the ceiling, inasmuch as the height of houses was increasing, and an upper storey was formed over the hall. In some cases, where vacant space per-

mitted, plaster ceilings, instead of being flat, were
carried up and formed into a large cove as is the case
at Herringstone in Dorset (Fig. 137), which is one of the

136. Parham, Sussex.   The Great Hall (1593).

most notable of its kind. The pattern is of the simplest,
but gains much character from being on the curve; the
main ribs are bent down at intervals, where they inter-
sect, to form the root of pendants which vary in their

forms.   The tympanum on the end wall, resulting from
the curves of the ceiling, is also ornamented with a
suitable pattern, and the cornice, making the circuit of
the room, binds the whole together with its strong
horizontal lines.   There is another fine coved ceiling at
Canons Ashby in Northamptonshire, differing in treat-

137. Herringstone, Dorset.
Coved Plaster Ceiling.

ment from this at Herringstone by reason of its being
curved all four ways, the point of intersection being
furnished with a large, open pendant.   The work in
these old ceilings is generally too irregular to suit the
correct taste of the modern workman, yet the effect is
softer and more pleasing than that of the mechanical
accuracy of the present day.

The variety of ornament in the ceilings of this period is extraordinary; sometimes it was merely a geometrical pattern duly repeated; sometimes a flowing pattern so varied that not a single portion of it occurs twice, save that the two halves of the ceiling are repeated in reverse fashion. Then, again, there is a strong simple framework with all the interspaces decorated either with floral ornament or subjects of natural history, or, still oftener, heraldic devices. As Gray says, in those days they employed the power of fairy hands

138. Apethorpe Hall, Northamptonshire.

Plaster Panel, from Ceiling, with
Arms of James I.

"To raise the ceiling's fretted height,
Each panel with achievements clothing."

This, it is true, is a poetic licence, for the panels seldom exhibited more than the family cognizance or coat-of-arms. The achievement, that is the shield, crest, mantling, and supporters, was reserved for very special cases, such as is shown in the fine panel of the royal arms of James I. from Apethorpe Hall in Northamptonshire (Fig. 138).

In spite of the elaboration of the detail, the general effect of these ceilings was quiet; and the same may be said of the wall panelling. To prevent monotony or tameness of appearance, a handsome treatment was often bestowed on special features, such as doorways and chimney-pieces, more particularly the latter. The

139. Wolveton House, Dorsetshire.

Interior, showing Doorway, Chimney-piece, and Ceiling.

doorways were frequently emphasised by pilasters and cornice; in the great hall the screen was elaborately decorated with panels, pilasters, and cornice. Heraldry was again brought in to aid the effect, thus at once

N

gratifying the foible of family pride, and imparting an air of dignity and splendour to the room. The chimney-piece was nearly always finely treated, whether it was of wood or of stone. Columns, pilasters, or grotesques supported a lofty shelf above the vast fireplace; over the shelf the design extended itself upwards with large panels, fantastic pilasters, and elaborate ornament till it was crowned with a cornice supporting, or seeming to support, the ceiling itself (Fig. 139). Heraldry, mythology, pedantry, sententiousness, all went to adorn the chimney-piece. The family arms, or incidents from a classic tale, or virtues personified, supplied the chief interest, while pithy inscriptions, generally in Latin, added a touch of that learning which was supposed to be the possession of all the well-to-do.

Shakespeare draws a picture of an Elizabethan room when he makes Iachimo describe Imogen's chamber :—

> " It was hanged
> With tapestry of silk and silver ; the story
> Proud Cleopatra when she met her Roman,
> And Cydnus swell'd above the banks, or for
> The press of boats or pride : a piece of work
> So bravely done, so rich, that it did strive
> In workmanship and value.

> " Her chimney
> Is south the chamber ; and the chimney-piece
> Chaste Dian, bathing ; never saw I figures
> So likely to report themselves.

> " The roof o' the chamber
> With golden cherubims is fretted ; her andirons
> (I had forgot them) were two winking Cupids
> Of silver, each on one foot standing, nicely
> Depending on their brands."

The drawing is true, with its tapestry, its chimney-piece, and its ceiling, all taking their inspiration from Italian sources. The "golden cherubims" are but a poetical version of the winged amorini of Italy.

The chimney-pieces of that time are as numerous as the fretted ceilings, and as varied in design. Many of them are of stone, still more of wood, and a few are of coloured marbles. In a large number the portion above the fireplace contains two panels, filled more often than

140. Stone Chimney-piece from Deene Park, Northamptonshire (1571).

not with shields of arms. One of these would bear the family coat simply; the other the quarterings of the owner at the time, or his own arms impaling those of his wife; these arms are frequently useful in identifying the builder of the house and in fixing its date. Sometimes the date itself was carved in a subsidiary panel, as is the case in the example from Deene Park (Fig. 140), which not only presents a fine display of heraldry, but bears the sententious inscription, " Amicus fidelis protexio fortis," and the date 1571. This chimney-piece is in stone ; a smaller one from a house in King's Lynn is in wood, and is dated 1623 (Fig. 141). The work, both in the panelling and carving, is excellent. Another

141. Wood Chimney-piece from a House at King's
Lynn (1623).

example in wood, of great elaboration, is from the hall of the butchers' guild in Hereford (Fig. 142).

Another of the special characteristics of houses of this period is the staircase. It has already been said that no examples are found previous to Elizabeth's time of anything but extremely simple stairs, generally of the corkscrew type, but sometimes consisting of straight flights in the thickness of a wall. These forms were

142. Wood Chimney-piece from the Hall of the Butchers'
Guild, Hereford.

still in use in the latter part of the sixteenth century:
Rothwell Market-house in Northamptonshire (1577) was
to have had a circular stair; and Hardwick Hall in

Derbyshire (1576) has nothing but plain flights of steps, nothing which can be considered an ornamental staircase.

143. Staircase, Crewe Hall, Cheshire.

But these were the exceptions; the rule was to have a broad staircase, generally of wood, with short runs of steps leading from landing to landing: the newel posts were stout and tall, and carried up well above the hand-rail, their tops being either wrought into striking shapes, or crowned with heraldic animals. When the staircase extended to many flights, the effect was very fine, as may be seen in the example from Crewe Hall (Fig. 143). The handrail was massive, and the space between it and the stout string was filled with thick turned balusters,

144. Staircase, with Dog-gate, Cold Overton, Leicestershire.

or occasionally with wood pierced in patterns. In a few instances a gate is to be found across the stairs, placed there to prevent dogs from roaming over the whole house. There is a good example at Hatfield House, and another at Cold Overton in Leicestershire (Fig. 144). At Rawdon House near Hoddesdon, there is a good staircase with heraldic newels and a pierced balustrade.

It leads up to a landing on which is an elaborate doorway of one of the principal chambers (Fig. 145). Innumerable other fine staircases might be mentioned, but these examples will suffice to indicate the style prevalent in the time of Elizabeth and James.

145. Staircase and Doorway, Rawdon House,
Hoddesdon, Hertfordshire.

These staircases led up to important rooms: to the great chamber and the long gallery, as well as to the bedrooms. The great chamber was a room of state, and answered somewhat to the drawing-room of the present day. It was, of course, decorated in the usual way with panelled walls, fretted ceiling, and a large chimney-piece. So, too, was the long gallery, perhaps the most characteristic room of an Elizabethan house. The earliest instance of a long gallery seems to have been at Hampton Court, of a date about 1540. It continued in fashion, designers vying in their endeavours

146. Astley Hall, Lancashire.
The Long Gallery.

to give it extraordinary length, until the time of Charles I., when, under the changed ideas as to household arrangement which then prevailed, it disappeared. Its precise object is not quite clear. At Apethorpe it was intended as a music-room, as testified by the inscription on the chimney-piece :—

" Rare and ever to be wisht maye sownde heere
Instruments wch fainte sprites and muses cheere,
Composing for the Body, Sowle, and Eare,
Which Sickness, Sadness, and Fowle Spirits feare."

Sir Henry Wotton, in his " Elements of Architecture," implies that it was a place for indoor exercise, for he says, in advising as to the aspect of the principal rooms of a house, that on the north side should be placed " all that are appointed for gentle motion, as galleries." It can hardly have been meant for pictures, as the fashion of collecting them and *articles de vertu* had not yet arisen. Galleries were generally lighted all down one side and at one or both ends ; indeed, continuous lighting was necessary, for their immense length would have rendered lighting from the ends only utterly futile. The illustration from Astley Hall, Lancashire (Fig. 146), gives a good idea of one of these rooms : it is probable, however, that its interest was originally enhanced by an elaborate plaster ceiling.

Most of the bedrooms, at any rate those of any importance, were decorated in the same way as the living rooms ; panelled walls, heraldic ceilings, and good chimney-pieces are still to be found in many bedrooms even of moderate size.

CHAPTER XI.

SEVENTEENTH CENTURY—PERSONAL DESIGN—TRANSITIONAL TREATMENT.

WITH the end of the second decade of the seventeenth century there opens a new chapter in English Architecture. Hitherto it had been largely impersonal; now it began to be personal, and its finest manifestations were henceforth to be linked with great names, with Inigo Jones, Sir Christopher Wren, Sir John Vanbrugh, and others. The main cause of the change is to be found in the pursuit of the Italian ideal. Up to this time the erection of houses and churches had not been thought of as "architecture," but merely as "building." The processes employed, both in regard to design and to construction, were the outcome of tradition. We have already seen how tradition had been modified in the sixteenth century by the introduction of Italian features, and the imperfect study of Italian models, in obedience to the prevailing fashion of the day, which demanded that particular form of decoration. But it must have been obvious to all instructed eyes that the efforts of English designers, so far as they aimed at a faithful transcript of the foreign copy, had been very wide of the mark. This was only to have been expected from the nature of the circumstances. There was no single mind at work controlling the whole of the design in all its branches. It is true that surveyors were employed to give a general superintendence. These men usually supplied a plan of the house, and not infrequently an elevation. This, at any rate, was the case during the reigns of Elizabeth and James, although there is little evidence that it had been the custom in earlier times. To the surveyors, of whom John Thorpe was the most remarkable, must accordingly be attributed the credit of the houses as a whole; of their arrangement, and of their general appearance. But the details of the treatment were left to artificers in the various trades, to the masons, the carpenters, the plasterers, and the plumbers. It is obvious that these men could not all be equally skilful, or equally conversant with the foreign fashion; and we may well be grateful that it was so, for from their diverse limitations sprang the quaint, piquant, and charming work of the period, endless in its variety yet throughout essentially English; in no other country is just the same development to be found.

But the tide of fashion was flowing strongly in the Italian direction. This can be gathered not only from the appearance of the work itself, and from subsequent developments, but from the drawings of Smithson, the surveyor (or architect), made about 1618, among which are designs for " Italyan wyndowes," " Italyan gates," an " Italyan grate," and a " pergular." Thorpe, although he had studied foreign books on architecture, and had made careful drawings of the " orders," makes no reference to " Italyan " features, nor do his details show anything like the same striving after " correct " design that is evident in Smithson's. A considerable number of young men travelled to Italy for the express purpose of studying the buildings of that country, some being sent thither by wealthy noblemen. A few of their names have been preserved, either through their having, like John Shute, published the results of their labours, or through their having written, as Charles Williams did to Sir John Thynne at Longleat, to offer their services in doing work "after the Italian fashion." But among all those who went none made such good use of his opportunities or was so gifted by nature to take advantage of them as Inigo Jones. It is to him that we owe the establishment of the matured Renaissance manner in England, the handling of Italian features with real knowledge and skill, the introduction of the full "Classic" style as distinguished from the tentative "Renaissance." With him, too, started the personal architecture of the designer who controlled the decoration throughout, as opposed to the impersonal architecture of the independent craftsmen who preceded him. The change was a momentous one; whether it resulted in a more pleasing type of building will probably always remain a matter of individual taste.

One notable result of the change was the dividing of house design into two streams : one academic and stately, the other traditional and homely. The one dealt with great mansions and public buildings, and was guided by men of eminence, who studied architecture as a fine art. The other dealt with the smaller houses, with schools, almshouses, and other buildings of less importance, and was guided by men of no especial culture, who probably underwent no more training than could be obtained in a builder's yard. Hence in out-of-the-way places houses may be found dated in the early years of the eighteenth century closely resembling those built in the early years of the seventeenth. But gradually the early traditions died out; the new classic manner permeated the whole of the building world, and even the smallest houses, so far as they had any pretensions to design at all, complied with the prevailing classic taste.

In the larger buildings there was a tendency to become more and more academic, to design more and more according to rule. Men of genius, like Inigo Jones

and Wren, bent these rules to their own purposes; but
their successors of the eighteenth century found it easier
to let the rules have the mastery, with the result that
much of their work is tame and insipid. At the same
time they pursued architecture in the abstract, without
due regard for its application to house design. The con-

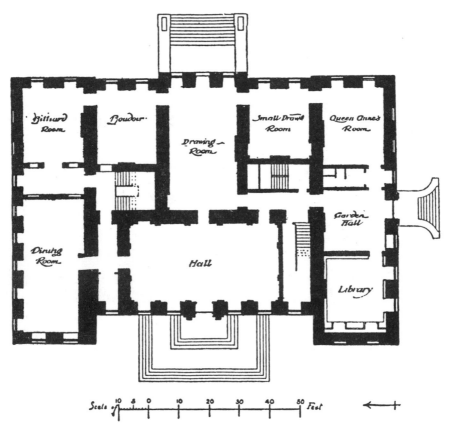

147. Plan of Raynham Park, Norfolk (*cir*. 1630-36).

sequence was that most of their efforts, although striking
as architectural compositions, are inconvenient as dwelling-houses. This point will be more fully dealt with in
its chronological order, meantime we must return on our
steps and take up the story where it was left at the close
of the reign of James I.

148. Raynham Park, Norfolk, The West Front.

The two tendencies in design just mentioned may already be observed during the lifetime of James, for in 1622 was built the Banqueting Hall at Whitehall, designed by Inigo Jones as part of a vast palace for the King, of which the rest was never undertaken. It is perhaps the most classic building of that century,

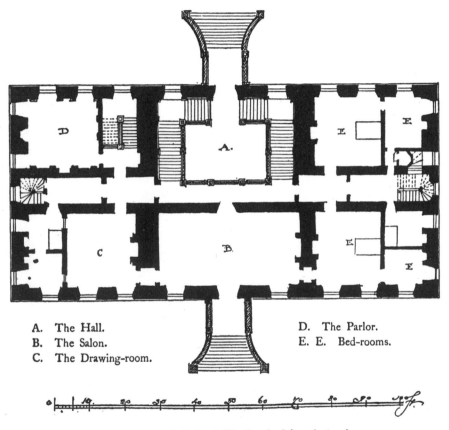

A. The Hall.
B. The Salon.
C. The Drawing-room.

D. The Parlor.
E. E. Bed-rooms.

149. Plan of Coleshill, Berkshire (1650).

quite devoid of any trace of Elizabethan detail. At the same time, and indeed for another ten or twelve years, were being built houses which still retained all the old characteristics. Such is Aston Hall, near Birmingham, which has the curved gables, the turrets, the chimneys, the mullioned windows, the ribbed ceilings, the busy

150. Coleshil House, Berkshire.

staircase, which had been customary in fine houses for the last fifty years. Yet Aston Hall was not completed till 1635. The most significant sign of change at Aston is the disposition of the hall, which, as already stated, is no longer intended as a living room, and is entered in the middle of its length instead of at one end through the customary screens. The change of habits which this alteration implies, coinciding as it did with the advent of more accurate knowledge of Italian ways, undoubtedly helped forward their establishment. It was no longer necessary to provide on the ground floor a great hall suitable for a living room, and dividing the family apartments from those where the servants worked and lived. The whole ground floor was devoted to the family, who were provided with a suite of salons surrounding the hall, which itself became a large vestibule leading to them. The servants were relegated to the basement ; not indeed for the first time, for Smithson has several plans in which this arrangement was adopted, and so has Thorpe ; but these were exceptions to the general rule. The long gallery and the great chamber went out of fashion. These rooms had been upstairs, the long gallery sometimes on the topmost floor, while not a few of the rooms on the ground floor had been "chambers" or "lodgings," that is in effect bedrooms. It now became more customary to devote the ground floor to the day-rooms, and the upper floor to bedrooms, especially in houses of medium size. In great mansions complete suites of living and sleeping rooms were still provided on the same floor. The plan of Raynham Park (Fig. 147), built according to various authorities either in 1630 or 1636, and attributed to Inigo Jones, shows the change that had taken place in domestic habits. So too does the plan of Coleshill in Berkshire (Fig. 149), built in 1650 from designs by the same master ; but in this case some of the ground-floor rooms are still intended to be used as bedrooms, and the dining-room is upstairs.

These two houses illustrate equally well the new methods adopted in treating the exterior. Elizabethan and Jacobean houses were picturesque and busy in their appearance owing to the varied outline of their plan, and to their irregular and broken sky-line caused by the gables, turrets, and chimneys with which they were furnished. The many lights of the mullioned windows also added much to their lively effect, while bay win-

151. Houses in High Street, Southwark.
(Now destroyed.)

dows were used with great skill to give rhythm and interest to the design.

The two most distinctive characteristics of the new style were the absence of gables and the substitution of sash windows for the old mullioned form.   Both these changes had a sobering effect on the appearance of a house.   In the absence of gables roofs had to be hipped, thus compelling a greater simplicity in their plan, and a much plainer sky-line.   The sash window was more stubborn of treatment than the mullioned window.   The latter could be either lengthened or widened by a row of lights and yet be in harmony with its neighbours; the sash window was not susceptible of such variation; it had to be of the same width and height as others of the same range.   For these reasons it lent itself ill to the forming of bay windows; it was too wide and too high, and altogether too large a feature to be adapted to the purpose, and accordingly bay windows went out of fashion.   The elements of design being thus greatly restricted, they required much skilful handling, and a keen sense of proportion to render the result satisfactory. It was just in these points that Inigo Jones's natural gifts and careful training enabled him to succeed.

Raynham Park (Fig. 148) is a link between the two styles; its projecting wings, finished with gables, are reminiscent of the past; its sash windows and its bold, carefully profiled cornice are a foretaste of the future. Coleshill (Fig. 150) has left Elizabethan times far behind, and retains nothing of their peculiarities either in plan or appearance.   There are no gables, the roof is hipped at each corner and starts from a widely projecting cornice.   The chimneys are gathered into large stacks, symmetrically placed; not into groups of single, slender shafts.   The dormers have no stonework about them; they belong to the roof, not to the walls.   The designer, having eschewed picturesque details, had to rely for his effect upon proportion and the careful spacing of his windows. Coleshill may be regarded as typical of the style adopted for large country houses down to the end of the seventeenth century. Up Park, Squerries, Melton Constable, and many others built towards the close of this century or in the first years of the next, are of the same type, although somewhat varied in treatment. There were many intermediate steps between Jacobean

152. Swakeleys, Middlesex (*cir.* 1630).

houses and houses like Coleshill. Some of these steps have been attributed to Inigo Jones himself—taken by him, the chroniclers assert, before his visit to Italy. Such are St John's College, Oxford, and the house at Houghton Conquest, in Bedfordshire, built for the Countess of Pembroke, "Sidney's sister, Pembroke's mother." But expert opinion is now inclined to doubt the correctness of such attribution. If Inigo Jones made no use of a transitional style, others did so.

Swakeleys in Middlesex (Fig. 152) is a case in point. Here mullioned windows are still retained, but the cornices, breaking out into pediments, and the gables crowned also with pediments, indicate the impending change.

153. Houses in Great Queen Street, Lincoln's Inn Fields (1640).
(From a Drawing by J. Nash, about 1840.)

It would seem as though the small size of the lights of mullioned windows had begun to be irksome before the solution of the difficulty by the adoption of sash windows. Accordingly round-headed lights of double the usual width were sometimes introduced among the small oblong lights, as may be seen in the drawing of

154. Sparrow's House, Ipswich.

the house of wood and plaster which formerly stood in High Street, Southwark (Fig. 151). Gables are still retained here, and also the old fashion of bringing forward the upper storeys beyond the lower. But indications of the change to a later treatment are to be found not only in the round-headed lights with their wood key-stones,

155. Cold Overton Hall, Leicestershire.
(Late in first half of 17th cent.)

but in the character of the ornamental plasterwork. If this street front is compared with that in Great Queen Street, Lincoln's Inn Fields, by John Webb (Fig. 153), the completeness of the impending change will be more readily grasped. In the later example there are no gables, no mullioned windows, no lead-lights. Instead we have a well-developed classic cornice with a row of dormers above it, sash windows, and bold pilasters, carefully proportioned. If again Sparrow's House at Ipswich (Fig. 154) were remodelled, as alleged, subse-

156. The Vicarage, Burford, Oxfordshire (dated 1672).

quently to the Restoration, it is a striking instance of the survival of the old-fashioned methods of treatment. But in the absence of any definite evidence it is probable that whatever was done in the time of Charles II., including the modelling of his arms in plaster, was merely a renovation. In style, at any rate, it is a step later than the house in Southwark. The windows in both cases are of the same family, but instead of the walls being finished by gables, they are crowned with a heavy classic cornice.

Another example of the transition is to be seen at Cold Overton in Leicestershire (Fig. 155), an interesting although somewhat plain house built among the grassy slopes beloved of hunting men. Here the mullioned windows are survivals from the ancient ways ; even more so is the projecting porch, with its round-arched door-way flanked by columns and surmounted by a four-light window ; while the plain flat bands which replace the old profiled strings, and the wide, flat-pitched gable belong to the newer methods of design. The date of this house is not known, but it must be in the earlier half of the century, and some of the work inside, notably the staircase with its dog-gate (Fig. 144), is frankly Jacobean in character. The survival of old ways in remote places is well shown in the vicarage at Burford in Oxfordshire, a house dated 1672 (Fig. 156). Here there is no attempt at pronounced classic. The roof is gabled, it has no cornice of any account ; the windows are mullioned, and the dormers retain some of the fantastic curls of the early years of the century. Nevertheless, in the plainness and precision of the whole treatment, in the flat shape of the mullions, and in the ovals of the dormers, the experienced eye can detect the march of Time. When it is remembered that this house was built when Wren was in the midst of his career, it will be realised how distinct were the two streams of design already alluded to—the stately, guided by great artists ; the homely, guided by unknown artisans.

CHAPTER XII.

CLASSIC DETAIL ESTABLISHED—INFLUENCE OF THE AMATEURS.

THE Civil War diverted men's thoughts from house-building, and inclined them rather in the opposite direction of destruction. The middle of the century was accordingly not prolific in examples of domestic architecture. Inigo Jones himself was hampered in his career by the part he was obliged to take in public affairs and by the disturbed state of the times. He was among those who surrendered at the fall of Basing House, and must have heard with regret of the order for "slighting" so interesting an old building. But many another ancient seat shared the same fate, to the great prejudice of the modern student of architecture.

With the Restoration, however, matters improved, and Charles II., in the intervals of more congenial pursuits, was regarded as a great patron of the arts, among which architecture now took a recognised place in English opinion. Many books had been published on the subject, especially in Italy. Some of these treatises had already been translated into English sixty or seventy years earlier, but they had not been studied with full effect. The efforts of Inigo Jones towards a purer taste were highly appreciated by men of culture like John Evelyn, and it became fashionable among the elect to study building from the somewhat new point of view of architecture. The only means of becoming acquainted with the art was through books, all of which derived their ultimate inspiration from the ancient

Roman, Vitruvius.   Already, in the second quarter of the century, Sir Henry Wotton had written a sensible treatise on the " Elements of Architecture," and now the same subject was undertaken by Evelyn.   The Italian authorities, who were his guides, as they had been Wotton's, had taken Vitruvius as their high priest, and the old buildings of Italy as their ensamples.   Within the pale of their cult, therefore, came no Gothic at all. Evelyn, accordingly, has no words too damnatory of Gothic buildings.   Barbarous nations, he says, destroyed the glorious Roman empire together with its stately monuments, " introducing in their stead, a certain fantastical and licentious manner of building, which we have since called modern (or Gothic rather): congestions of heavy, dark, melancholy, and monkish piles, without any just proportion, use, or beauty, compared with the truly ancient."   Instead of the " beautiful orders," he says, they set up " slender and misquine pillars, or rather bundles of staves, and other incongruous props, to support incumbent weights and ponderous arched roofs, without entablature."   He begs any man of judgment to compare Henry VII.'s Chapel at Westminster, with its " sharp angles, jetties, narrow lights, lame statues, lace, and other cut-work and crinkle crankle," with Inigo Jones's Banqueting Hall, or what was then being advanced by Sir Christopher Wren at St Paul's; and then to " pronounce which of the two manners strikes the understanding as well as the eye with the more majesty and solemn greatness."   The whole of the ancient cathedrals of England and the Continent, mentioning the most famous by name, he dismisses as " mountains of stone, vast and gigantic buildings indeed; but not worthy the name of Architecture."

Here we have a vast change from fifty years earlier. Thorpe and Smithson came under the Italian influence, especially the latter; but both of them thought Henry

VII.'s Chapel worthy of study.   Each of them has a plan of it among his drawings ; and Smithson has a plan of some of the vaulting as well, not to mention an outline drawing of a Gothic window.   The Italianising of English taste had indeed progressed when we find an architectural guide placing not only Henry VII.'s Chapel, but all Gothic work, outside the domain of architectural study.   But outside it was, and there it remained until the commencement of the nineteenth century, when the publications of Carter, Britton, and others began to awaken interest in it.

The pursuit of architecture now became an elegant accomplishment, and it fell largely into the hands of amateurs.   Books in plenty gave precise rules for its treatment.   Any one gifted with a modicum of taste could design a facade ; and if he followed his rules his proportions would probably be not unpleasing.   If he had some inventive faculty and were sufficiently bold, he could produce a group of buildings that should have a striking and even noble effect.   This was indeed the weakness of the whole system.   Designing became a striving after external effect without paying due regard to the purpose of the building.   The large houses of the time of the first two Georges are magnificent to look at, but uncomfortable to live in.   Everything is sacrificed to the state apartments.   Most of these are noble rooms admirably adapted for stately functions ; but the ordinary living rooms are mean in comparison, and are not contrived, whether as to aspect, position, or their relation one to the other, in order to make for cheerfulness or comfort.   In towns, where space was restricted, a more simple treatment was adopted, and extravagance eschewed.   This resulted in such plain but well-proportioned houses as Newcastle House, in Lincoln's Inn Fields (Fig. 157), designed for Lord Powys by Captain

Wynne in 1686.   It has, however, lost much of its character by the removal of the stone cornice which originally surmounted the windows of the second floor.

One of the favourite devices of the time for producing a splendid group was to place the principal rooms in a lofty central block, to flank it on either side

157. Newcastle House, Lincoln's Inn Fields, London (1686).

with a block of subsidiary rooms at some distance, and to connect these outlying wings with the main building by colonnades.   As a rule one wing contained the kitchens and the other the stables.   Two inconveniences must have followed from this arrangement: the stables were too near the house, the kitchens too far off.   Sir

Henry Wotton had already uttered a warning against placing the kitchen at a great distance from the dining-room, "or else, besides other inconveniences, perhaps some of the dishes may straggle by the way." Inigo Jones appears to have been the first to adopt this wide-spreading disposition at Stoke Bruerne in Northampton-shire, a house of which the central block has been burnt down; his successors bettered his example, followed it with frequency, and established a fashion which survived till late in the eighteenth century.

In Isaac Ware's "Complete Body of Architecture," written for students of the art, and published in 1756, several chapters of the third book are devoted to explaining how a house of this kind should be designed. The author supposes a gentleman with a moderate family to be desirous of building a house in the country "without columns, or other expensive decorations"; handsome, though not pompous. Having selected a site in accordance with principles previously enunciated by Mr Ware, the gentleman asks a builder how much ground the house ought to cover to meet his require-ments. The builder at once replies that a 65 ft. frontage will answer the purpose. Although the steps by which this rapid decision is arrived at are not indicated, it seems to be satisfactory as well as inevitable. Sixty-five feet being the correct length of the front, it follows that from 40 to 45 ft. must be the depth. The intention being to achieve something handsome (though not pompous), the kitchen is not to be put under the parlour, nor the stable in the corner of the yard: "a bricklayer could do that." These offices are to be placed in detached wings, "so that from a plain design, such as the vulgar builder would have proposed, here shall arise, with little more expense, a centre, its wings, and their communication." The position of the detached wings is next to be

settled. In order to be proportionate with a centre of
65 ft. frontage, it would appear that the wings should
start 28 ft. away to the right and left; as to their
distance frontwards from the centre, the author is not
so certain, but he advises 13 ft. Then comes the actual
size of the wings, which must correspond exactly with
one another, although one is to contain the kitchen and
the other the stables. The best measure in proportion
to the 65 ft. is 35 : accordingly that is to be the length of
the front of each wing. As to their depth, "for a house
of this bigness and design, 48 ft. will be a good measure."
The size of the three blocks being thus settled on these
somewhat arbitrary lines, the architect is to proceed to
the construction and distribution of the rooms, bearing
in mind that it is "always best to accommodate the
inner distribution of a house to the outer aspect when
that can conveniently be done." But as the author
admits that tastes may vary and occasions alter the
choice, he proceeds in different chapters to set forth
different ways in which his spaces may be divided up
into rooms. Into these details we need not enter, but
it is evident that the gentleman with the moderate
family would have to keep his personal predilections
as to aspect, prospect, the relation of rooms one to the
other, and other matters incidental to comfort, strictly
in subjection, in order not to conflict with the proportions and outlines laid down by his architect.

The study of architecture as an art governed by rules
and founded on proportion has carried us a long way
from mediæval methods, which led to rooms being
placed where they were wanted without regard to
regularity of appearance; and almost as far from the
ways of the Elizabethan designer, who contrived to get
the requisite accommodation in its traditional relationship within his symmetrical outline. The former sub-

ordinated appearance to convenience ; the latter regarded them as of equal importance ; the eighteenth-century preceptor made convenience bow to his duly proportioned outline.

Mr Ware gives a plan and elevation of his design (Fig. 158), but with the wings rather more distant from

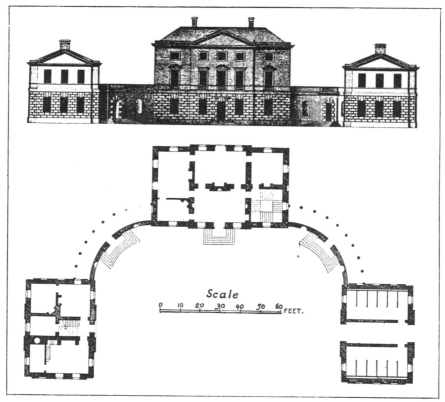

158. Plan and Elevation of a House.
From Isaac Ware's "Complete Body of Architecture" (1756).

the house than he at first suggested. The left-hand block contains the kitchens, the right-hand the stables. Of the six ground-floor windows in the outlying blocks, the exigencies of internal arrangement require that four should be shams, although they are in the forefront of his architectural composition ; and it is probable that some of the upper windows followed suit. The route

P

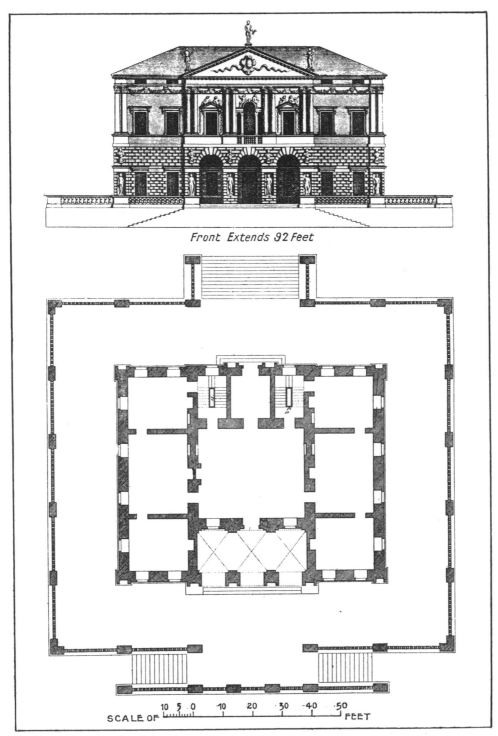

Front Extends 92 Feet

159. Plan and Elevation of a House.

From Kent's " Designs of Inigo Jones."

from the kitchen to the dining-room lies across a lobby, a room, and 50 ft. of open arcade before it arrives at the outer wall of the central house wherein the dining-room is situated. When these and other inconveniences are borne in mind, it is manifest that such principles of design could have no lasting vitality.

Mr Ware, writing in the middle of the eighteenth century, was only following in the footsteps of his eminent guides of thirty years earlier. Whether we look at the house designs of Inigo Jones through the eyes of Kent in 1727, or those of Gibbs through his own eyes in 1728, we find formal arrangements aiming at, and often achieving stateliness, but at much sacrifice of household comfort. Kent's "Designs of Inigo Jones," many of which probably owe their special characteristics as much to himself as to the great master, consist of a series of plates giving plans and elevations; an explanatory "Table" precedes them. The elucidatory matter is confined to a few lines, such as those to plate 15 of vol. ii. (Fig. 159). "The Plan of the first Story with the Elevation of the principal Front of a House, with an Arcade, standing on a Terras, about which is a Ballustrade. The Rooms of the Plan are 18 Feet high; those above 'em are 16 Feet high, except the Middle Room which comes over the Arcade to the Front, and includes the *Attic* Story. The Windows of the *Attic* Story are in the Frieze of the Entablature that encompasses the Building." There are three points to be remarked here. First, the importance attached to the heights of the rooms. Secondly, that the "middle room" includes the attic storey; it became fashionable (at any rate in published plans) to have one large and lofty room, sometimes as much as 40 ft. high. Thirdly, that the windows of the attic storey are in the frieze of the entablature: this would allow a width of 3 or 4 ft., by a height which could

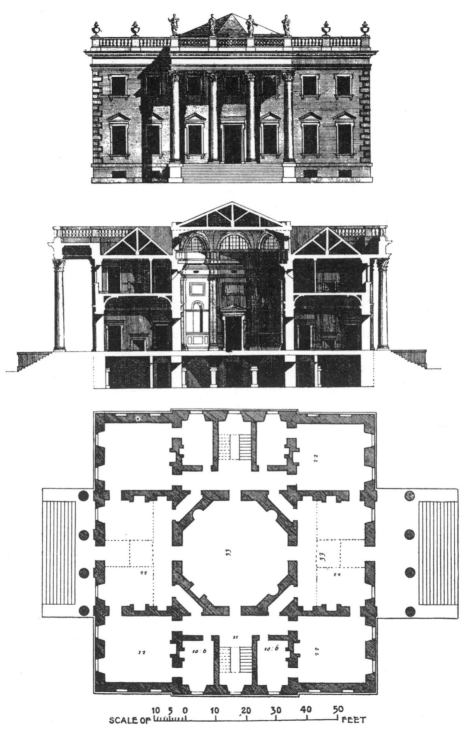

160. Plan, Elevation, and Section of a House.
From Gibbs's " Book of Architecture," 1728.

only be measured in inches, for the windows of rooms of considerable area—a complete sacrifice of internal comfort for the sake of external effect. But no doubt, as such rooms were only "lodgings for servants," they were considered good enough. Kent explains on another plate that the lodging rooms for servants "receive their light from the hall, whose top rises in a pavilion above the roof."

Kent gives this as one of Inigo Jones's own designs; it may be in reality Jones revised by Kent; but in any case the master's reputation rests on surer ground. The illustration is offered not as a specimen of Inigo Jones's work, but of what the early eighteenth century regarded as a suitable and elegant piece of domestic architecture. The attic storey, here starved of light, was a considerable trouble to designers. Its space was necessary in order to get sufficient accommodation, partly owing to the fact of the great room occupying two floors; and much ingenuity was brought to bear upon the problem of lighting it without overloading the elevation with windows. One method was this of squeezing them into the frieze. Another was to light it from the roof where hidden from observation. Another was to borrow light from the upper part of the central lofty room. This device is adopted in connection with the passages of Gibbs's design in Fig. 160, which also gives a good idea of the manner in which the central hall was treated.

Such lofty rooms as this hall, lighted from windows at their summit, and warmed (if they ever got warm) by a single fire, must have been much more magnificent than comfortable. In large houses vast rooms had their uses; they could be opened on state occasions and left for more homely apartments in the intervals; but both in Kent's book and in Gibbs's they occur in houses of moderate size, and could hardly have been left out of account in daily life.   They go to show what importance was attached to state and dignity by every " person of quality."

Campbell's designs were actuated by similar motives. In his "Vitruvius Britannicus," published in 1717, he describes a small essay of his invention for the ingenious gentleman, Tobias Jenkyns, Esq.   On the " first storey, extending 120 foot," he says, " here is the double and single cube, the hall being 27 by 54 ; here is 18 by 27, which is the *sesqui altera*, and 21 by 27, the *sesqui tertia*, and you pass gradually from the larger to the lesser."   The front was to have " a rustic basement and two orders of pilasters in the theatrical, which admits of more gaiety than the temple or palatial style."

Such were the principles underlying the house design of professed masters in architecture in the first half of the eighteenth century, and it was by publishing their designs that they commended themselves to the public. They had travelled far from the virility of Inigo Jones and the splendid common-sense of Wren.   Not that Wren had left much of a legacy in house design.   He was an architect of the first rank, but his work had been chiefly concerned with St Paul's Cathedral in London, with the city churches, with palaces and public buildings. There are but few houses among his preserved drawings, and what there are throw little illumination on the subject ; he never pursued it so as to make it his own. A few houses here and there are attributed to him, but it has always been the fashion to attribute unknown work of exceptional merit to some master of the period on little or no sound authority.   But although he left no direct legacy, a man of such wealth in architectural power could hardly die and leave nothing behind him ; and doubtless to his influence may be traced much of the spirit which characterises the vernacular work of the eighteenth century.

CHAPTER XIII.

Eighteenth-Century Exteriors—The Palladian Style.

ARCHITECTURAL design having become an elegant occupation founded on so impracticable a basis, it is not surprising to find it pursued by amateurs. Lord Burlington was the most eminent of these, and he tried his hand, according to contemporary accounts, at a number of houses as well as at some semi-public buildings, such as the Assembly Room at York. Kent includes several in his book on Inigo Jones, where they suffer somewhat by comparison with the genuine work of the master. The well-known house in Burlington Street for General Wade was another of his creations, of which Walpole recounts that being ill-contrived and inconvenient, yet having a beautiful front, Lord Chesterfield said that as the General could not live in it to his ease, he had better take a house over against it and look at it. The villa at Chiswick was yet another of his designs, borrowed, as Walpole says, from a villa of Palladio's. Though faulty in plan and arrangement, as that chronicler admits, yet these blemishes could not "depreciate the taste that reigns in the whole." He then adds an observation which throws much light on the motives that underlay the architectural design of the time. "The larger court," he says, "dignified by picturesque cedars, and the classic scenery of the small court that unites the old and the new house, are more worth seeing than many fragments of ancient grandeur, which our travellers visit under all the dangers attendant on long voyages." It would seem that to have a bit of architectural grouping that really reminded you of Italy more than compensated for damp, draughty, and inconvenient rooms.

Henry, Earl of Pembroke, according to Walpole, was another of the "men of the first rank who contributed to embellish their country by buildings of their own design in the purest style of antique composition." William, Earl Fitzwilliam, designed a new front to Wentworth Castle; General Conway erected a rustic bridge, of which every stone was placed by his own direction; but from a reference in one of Walpole's letters to George Montagu, it was hardly a piece of architecture, but rather a mere piling up of large stones; this, however, the writer regarded as much superior to a regular Palladian structure. Mr Chute, at his seat of the Vyne, in Hampshire, designed and erected a theatric staircase. Dean Aldrich and Dr Clarke at Oxford, and Sir James Burroughs at Cambridge, were also amateurs, but they appear to have had more claim as designers than some of those whom Walpole extols. The amateur architect of the eighteenth century had, indeed, a long and even illustrious ancestry. Already in Charles II.'s reign Sir John Denham, a poet, had been surveyor of the works to the King. Wren, who succeeded him, was himself an amateur, in the sense that he received no early training in architecture, and that his reputation as a scientist was fully established before he turned his attention to art. But Wren was a man of exceptional genius and capacity, and soon mastered the technicalities of his new calling. Sir John Vanbrugh was a poet before he was an architect, yet to him we owe houses of the first importance, such as Blenheim and Castle Howard. Besides these amateurs there were men who had received a definite training as architects, John Webb, the nephew and son-in-law of Inigo Jones; Nicholas

Hawksmoor, the assistant of Wren; James Gibbs; Colin Campbell; Thomas Ripley, of whom Walpole says that "in the mechanic part, and in the disposition of apartments and conveniences," he was superior to Lord Burlington himself; and William Kent, the protégé and friend of the same munificent and gifted nobleman. But even among these professional architects the amateur spirit prevailed, and their clients had to adapt themselves to the houses provided for them, instead of the houses being adapted to the wants of the clients.

Other designers might be named of this period and of the preceding half-century, as well as of later times, but the present object is to trace in a brief way the gradual changes which took place in houses themselves, without burdening the reader with many particulars concerning their architects. The immediate source of inspiration for all designers of this period was the Italian, Andreas Palladio; and no designation has been more aptly bestowed on a phase of architecture than Palladian upon that of the eighteenth century. Every type of plan that was employed, every type of elevation, almost every kind of feature that was adopted, has its prototype among Palladio's designs. In one instance, Mereworth "Castle" in Kent, Campbell, who designed it, states that he copied it from a villa by Palladio built near Vicenza for Signor Paolo Armerico. It is true that he introduced a few variations, but substantially it is the same design; a design which had already been adapted, with other variations, by the Earl of Burlington in his villa at Chis-. wick. This is the most notable instance of direct copyism; but a comparison of any of the published plans of that period with those given by Giacomo Leoni in his " Architecture of A. Palladio," will show that they were all founded on Italian models, and derived little (except the names of some of the rooms) from English tradition.

This planting of Italian villas on English soil, where they were subjected to a climate wholly different from that of the land of their origin; this handling of the plan and elevation with a view to architectural effect, instead of with a view to the comfort of daily life, was of a piece with the artificiality of the age in other directions. Among the letters of Sir Thomas Fitzosborne is one written in 1739 to a friend whom he designates Philotes. In it he describes how he had lately visited another friend (Euphronius), who was shortly going to the wars in Flanders. As the warrior was

161. House in St James's Square, London (1772).

not one of those who preserve the chance of fighting another day by running away, there was some probability of his never returning. Accordingly he had caused his portrait to be taken after a manner designed by his father-in-law. He was portrayed as Hector, his wife as Andromache, his sister-in-law and little boy as the nurse holding Astyanax. So much was the writer pleased with this "uncommon family-piece," that he could wish it were the fashion to have all such pictures executed in some such manner. Architects, it is clear, were not the only designers who drew their inspiration from classic sources.

But however mistaken their ideals were, the architects of George I.'s time went a long way towards achieving them. Stateliness within and without, noble proportions, careful and refined detail—all these they produced in plenty. Possibly their noble clients, the "persons of quality," the "persons of distinction," were satisfied with the results, and were content to forego the comforts of home for the opportunity of living the stately life. Yet from contemporary observers we get occasionally a word of protest. After hearing a description of Blenheim, Pope says,

> "'Tis very fine,
> But where d'ye sleep, or where d'ye dine?
> I see from all you have been telling
> That 'tis a house, but not a dwelling."

He tells Lord Burlington, too, that his noble rules would fill half the land with imitating fools, who, among other things,

> "Shall call the wind thro' long arcades to roar,
> Proud to catch cold at a Venetian door;
> Conscious they act a true Palladian part,
> And if they starve, they starve by rules of art."

The rules of art were supreme. They had achieved their supremacy by the time that George I. came to the throne. Inigo Jones was too original a thinker, too close to the old traditions, to be entirely fettered by them.

Wren was too powerful a genius, too much occupied in solving constructional problems, to become their slave. He was too busy surmounting real architectural difficulties to occupy his time in half-hearted attempts to translate Italian villas into terms of English mansions ; and some at least of his contemporaries refrained from the favourite pursuit of his successors. In the second half of the eighteenth century architects gave themselves

162. Boughton House, Northamptonshire (*cir.* 1700).

a little more freedom of treatment, while still conforming to the very careful proportions of the classic styles. The brothers Adam, for instance, while indulging in no great flights of fancy, bestowed great care on the proportions and the detail of their work. The house, No. 20 St James's Square (Fig. 161), is a good example of the refined manner of Robert Adam, although, compared with the productions of the early part of the century, it may be considered a little insipid.

Boughton House in Northamptonshire lies outside the usual run of classic houses of its period. It was built, or rather rebuilt, by Ralph, Duke of Montagu, who incorporated in his new house a considerable portion of his ancestral home, which had been first erected in the middle of the sixteenth century. Montagu had been ambassador at the court of Louis XIV., and on his return to England towards the end of the seventeenth century, he built his house, as one chronicler affirms, after the model of Versailles. It was a very modest version, it is true; but there is a French feeling about it, in rather refreshing contrast to the innumerable Palladian mansions of later years (Fig. 162). The "long arcade" is there, but there is a welcome absence of overpowering columns and cornices, and the windows are all adequate for their purpose. Its restrained treatment, indeed, leads the casual visitor to pronounce it dull; but its very simplicity produces dignity, and its detail is refined. Within, it has ranges of noble rooms (Fig. 183), which, like those at Hampton Court, have the drawback of leading one into the other without the help of a corridor. They are all panelled with large panels, and are full of fine furniture of the period, and fine pictures. There are several excellent staircases, of different and somewhat unusual design; and many of the ceilings exhibit the masterpieces of Verrio or his school (Fig. 209). The house was the centre of a vast and magnificent lay-out, in which great avenues, sunk gardens, canals, lakes, cascades, and statuary all played their part. The whole place, in spite of the decay of the gardens, retains much of its original interest, and gives a vivid idea of the home of a great noble of the time of William and Mary.

Another house with much work of the same period is Drayton, in the same county. This is an interesting edifice dating back to the beginning of the fourteenth

163. The Entrance, Drayton House, Northants (*cir.* 1700).

century. The early roof of the great hall has already been illustrated (Fig. 84). Considerable alterations were made in the reign of Henry VI.; a long wing was added in Elizabeth's time; and the close of the seventeenth century left perhaps the most lasting mark of all. The hall was refronted and furnished with a fine doorway (Fig. 163), and enormous sash windows. At the ends of the front courtyard columned arcades were introduced. A chapel was contrived against the ancient windowless wall of fortified times. Most of the old mullioned windows were replaced by sashes. Two venerable towers were crowned with cupolas on columns, which lift themselves up against the sky and proclaim the identity of the house at a glance. New staircases were contrived, one covered with a coved ceiling on which Lanseroon tried his skill. Many rooms were panelled with the large panels of the time. The long gallery in the attic of the Elizabethan wing was made into a library with rows of carefully designed shelves. A little room leading out of the library was fitted up as a boudoir for the Duchess of Norfolk; its ceiling was coved and gilt, and a mirror placed in the central panel; the walls were partly panelled and partly fitted with cases of curious Chinese objects; the floor was covered with a charming design in parquetry, where formal patterns were interspersed with dainty little birds, admirably drawn. The great hall was ceiled below the ancient open-timber roof. The whole place was renovated within and without, and newly furnished with fine chairs, settees, tables, and beds, which remain to this day in the house where they went when they were new. Nor was this all. The gardens were rearranged; stables were built; long walls of enclosure were raised, pierced with gateways into which splendid iron gates were hung. The front court was enclosed on one side with a long stretch of excellent iron railings. Quaint flights of steps led from one level to another. Innumerable lead urns, large and small, but all bearing delicately modelled designs, were placed at intervals along the balustrades, or mounted on great stone pedestals as worthy to form central objects in the various quarters of the garden. The whole place is another admirable example of how noblemen housed themselves in those days, and it has this advantage over Boughton, that it preserves its gardens, and that it has a longer and more varied history to look back upon.

Shortly after the work at Boughton and Drayton was finished, Sir John Vanbrugh was laying his " heavy loads " on the earth in various parts of the country. Heavy they may be, but no one can deny them vigour and force. Vanbrugh, like his contemporaries, troubled himself little about the niceties of planning from the point of view of daily life, nor did he even provide rooms of a size and dignity proportionate to the vast palaces he designed. But no architect of the time succeeded better in pleasing the passer-by with his stately buildings. Blenheim, the gift of a grateful nation to her most distinguished hero, was rivalled by Castle Howard (Fig. 164), the private enterprise of a wealthy nobleman. Eastbury in Dorset was nearly as large, and from the outset must have been something of a white elephant to its owners. At the end of the eighteenth century its possessor is said to have offered an annuity of £200 to any one who would live there and keep it in repair. Finding nobody willing to undertake the responsibility, he finally pulled down all but one wing. Seaton Delaval, in Northumberland, though not so large, was still on an extravagant scale. The central block, a fine and massive piece of building, had nevertheless no great amount of accommodation,

164. Castle Howard, Yorkshire (1714).

and it has never been rebuilt since it was burnt down in 1752. Both the outlying wings remain ; the kitchen was in one, many yards distant from the dining-room ; and some of the bedrooms in this block have to this day no direct communication with the outer air. The other wing contained, as usual, the stables ; but so vast are its spaces that the standings within it that are used have had to be enclosed in order to keep them warm.

The plan of Castle Howard (Fig. 165) shows what splendour Vanbrugh and his clients aimed at. The house itself, with a long extending garden front, a lofty hall, and the prevalent curved colonnades flanking the chief entrance, is supported by two projecting wings, containing on one side the chapel, and on the other the kitchen and other rooms called the " hunting apartments." Outside each wing is a large court—the stable court on one side, the kitchen court on the other, the whole disposition producing a frontage of 660 feet. Blenheim by the same reckoning extended 850 feet. The bird's-eye view of Castle Howard (Fig. 164) shows the stately treatment of the exterior seen from the front ; while Fig. 166 (from a photograph) shows the garden façade. It is a palace rather than a private house. The general view also shows how the buildings that compose the wings are treated absolutely alike, although their purposes are widely different. This practice must have resulted in extravagance and inconvenience at one end or the other, probably at both. Doubtless this aspect of the question occurred to the designer, but it must be remembered that the early eighteenth century frankly built for show rather than for use. Pope points this moral in his letter to Burlington—

" You show us Rome was glorious, not profuse,
And pompous buildings once were things of use."

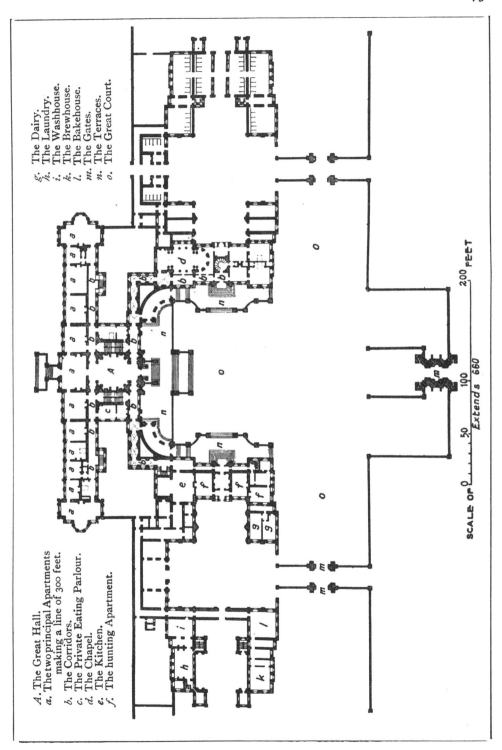

A. The Great Hall.
a. The two principal Apartments making a line of 300 feet.
b. The Corridors.
c. The Private Eating Parlour.
d. The Chapel.
e. The Kitchen.
f. The hunting Apartment.

g. The Dairy.
h. The Laundry.
i. The Washhouse.
k. The Brewhouse.
l. The Bakehouse.
m. The Gates.
n. The Terraces.
o. The Great Court.

SCALE OF 0   50   100   200 FEET
Extends 660

165. Castle Howard, Yorkshire.   Plan of Principal Floor.

The settled proportions in which architects then delighted, the double cube, Campbell's *sesquialtera* and *sesquitertia*, resulted in fine apartments, of which the double cube room at Wilton in Wiltshire is the most notable.   There is another room of similar proportions, but rather smaller, in the same county, in the Bishop's palace at Salisbury.   This is the drawing-room, built over some of Bishop Poore's twelfth-century vaulting. It is 50 ft. by 25 ft., a fine apartment, well adapted for the semi-private functions which diversify the daily life of a great Church dignitary, but perhaps a little too large for ordinary family use.   On the opposite side of the close is a house which aptly illustrates the type of plan familiar in the architectural folios of the time.   It is a large square house of almost stately appearance. A flight of steps leads up to the spacious entrance hall, which is two storeys high, and contains an excellent staircase.   Straight across the hall is the dining-room, of reasonable size.   To the left lies a room which extends the whole depth of the house from front to back, a distance of between 30 and 40 ft., while its width is not quite half as much.   There can be little doubt that the room is too long for its width, and that there would have been more comfort had the architect been less ambitious.   For the purposes of daily life the occupants prefer a smaller room on the other side of the hall.   The bedrooms are few in number, and the actual accommodation of the house is by no means so large as its appearance suggests, much space being sacrificed for the hall.

Another example of the fine houses of the eighteenth century is Campbell's Wanstead in Essex (Fig. 167), built shortly before 1720.   In his "Vitruvius Britannicus" he gives three designs for this house, two in the first volume and one in the third.   The second design, some-

166. Castle Howard, Yorkshire. The Garden Façade.

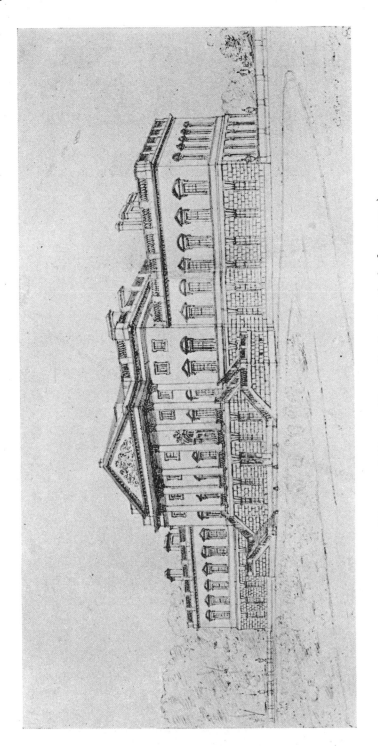

167. Wanstead House, Essex (built shortly before 1720).

what modified in detail, was carried out ; these modifications are shown on the third design, which also includes a tower at each end of the façade ; it was, however, quite as well that these towers were not built, for they would have been no improvement. The view here given was taken from the house itself, which was pulled down in 1822. It is a dignified composition, one of the least extravagant of its period, but the plan, although more compact than many, is ill-adapted for the ordinary routine of household life.

If we leave the architecture of the masters and of their books, and turn to the ordinary houses of the time, we find something much more home-like and convenient. These smaller houses reflect, though dimly, the stately handling of their more pompous contemporaries. They are generally a complete and symmetrical whole, and if in the course of time their owners wish to enlarge them, it becomes a problem of some difficulty how to do so without spoiling their appearance. The entrance door is in the middle of one front, and is flanked on either hand by three or four sash windows, spaced so as to fall into groups. The group over the door is often surmounted by a pediment, or has some special treatment, as at Rothwell manor house (Fig. 192). The angles of the building generally have quoins, the roof is hipped every way, and at the eaves there is a projecting cornice of varying degrees of richness. The chimneys are gathered together in large solid stacks ; the roof surface is broken by dormers. The whole effect is simple and quiet. The large spaces of plain walling, the large area of the window openings, the large chimney-stacks are all in complete contrast to the lively windows, steep gables, and detached chimney-shafts of Elizabethan and Jacobean houses. There are innumerable examples of this kind throughout the country. Every old-fashioned town has two or three, occupied by leading inhabitants, the doctor, the solicitor, the maiden ladies. Not a few manor houses are of the same type, with rooms of reasonable size and height, and the eating-room within easy reach of the kitchen. A good specimen of a small house is Fenton House, Hampstead, of which the plan is given in Fig. 168, and the side elevation in Fig. 169. The plan is compact

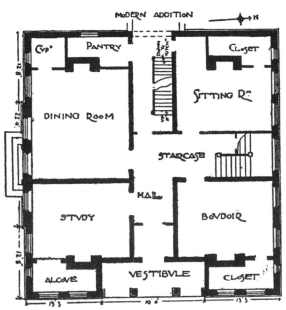

168. Fenton House, Hampstead.
Ground Plan.

and well arranged, there is no attempt at grandeur, and the rooms are accordingly disposed with a view primarily to comfort; yet both within and without the effect is handsome; there is nothing pretentious on the one hand, nor mean and makeshift on the other. The elevation follows the usual simple lines mentioned above.

It is seldom that these houses are dated, and they have not been considered of sufficient importance for any one to record the year of their building; it is therefore not possible to place the examples here illustrated in chronological order, except in the case of the house at Burwash in Sussex (Fig. 170), which bears the date 1699 in a plaster panel on the soffit of the hood over the front door. Two features which agree with the date, and place it earlier than the other examples, are the wood mullioned windows and the panelled chimneys. The next three illustrations (Figs. 171, 172, 173) were probably all built during the first quarter of the eighteenth century. They have sash windows of which the wood casing forms a broad white margin to the opening. One has architraves to its windows, one merely keystones by way of ornament, and one has no relief of this kind. Varieties such as these, unpretending as they are, impart a certain

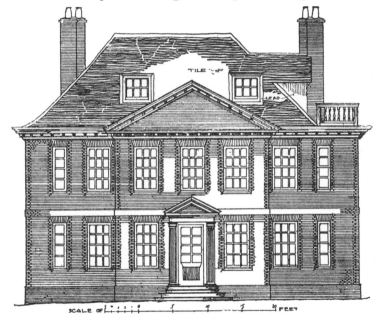

169. Fenton House, Hampstead.
Side Elevation.

amount of character. The remaining two examples (Figs. 174, 175) date from towards the end of the century. They show how formal and spiritless house design was growing. The absence of a wide overhanging cornice seems to deprive them of half their character. On the other hand, they are too simple and unpretentious to excite that active dislike which some of the more laboured houses of yet later times arouses.

The iron gates and railings of the period from

170. " Roppynden," Burwash, Sussex (1699).

171. The Rectory House, Burford, Oxfordshire.

172. House at Horsham, Sussex.

173. Heale House, Middle Woodford, near Salisbury

174. House at Faversham (late 18th cent.).

175. House at Colchester (late 18th cent.).

William III. to George II. afford some of the finest specimens of craftsmanship which the country can boast. Those at Drayton House have already been mentioned. They were mostly wrought for the Duchess of Norfolk about the year 1700, and much of the work bears her monogram. From the wealth of examples which the gardens and park offer, two have been selected, one from the side of the front court (Fig. 176), and one from the broad avenue which runs westward from the entrance front (Fig. 177). In the former the device of placing the massive hammered leafage in the tympanum of the arch, with the bright sky as a background, is singularly happy. In the latter the combination of the delicate ironwork with the lofty

176. Drayton House, Northamptonshire.
Gates in the Side of Fore-court (*cir.* 1700).

177. Drayton House.
Gates at the End of the West Avenue (*cir.* 1700).

stone piers crowned with large lead urns produces a noble effect, which is heightened by the remote position of the group from the house at the end of an avenue never meant for traffic. It was only a lordly munificence which could place so notable a feature where in the ordinary way it would be but dimly visible.

At Eaton Hall in Cheshire is another fine example (not, however, in its original position) of somewhat unusual design (Fig. 178). Here, too, the more elaborate

178. Gates at Eaton Hall, Cheshire.

part of the work is high up, where it now shows against the sky; the lower parts are plain, and veil, without obscuring, the view. The pillars instead of being in stone are built up of ironwork. Clever as the idea is, the effect is not so monumental as when the delicacy of the metal is bounded by the solidity of stone or brick.

There is a splendid range of gates and railing at Carshalton in Surrey, erected in 1723 (Fig. 179) as part

179. Railings and Gates at Carshalton House, Surrey (1723).

of the embellishments of the gardens and park of Carshalton House, which was to have been built for Sir Thomas Scawen from the designs of Giacomo Leoni. It never was built, however, and these gates (of which the designer is not known), together with some others of less pretension, and a bridge, are all that remain of an ambitious scheme. The stone piers at either end, surmounted by lively lead figures, help the monumental effect, an effect which would perhaps have been even finer had the range of ironwork not been quite so long.

180. Gate to a House in High Street, Richmond, Surrey.

But it was not only large houses to which these fine adjuncts were applied. The neighbourhood of London abounds in charming specimens attached to houses of quite small size, such as that in Fig. 180; and even in London itself there are still left interesting examples, many of them yet retaining the extinguisher used by the linkboys after piloting their patrons through the difficulties of the dark and ill-paved streets.

CHAPTER XIV.

LATE SEVENTEENTH AND EIGHTEENTH CENTURIES—INTERIORS—DETAILS AND FEATURES.

THE gradual change in character which has been traced in the external treatment of houses of the later part of the seventeenth century and of the eighteenth is also to be found in the internal decoration. The exuberant and vivacious detail of Elizabethan and Jacobean work gave way to the more sober and scholarly rendering of Inigo Jones, Webb, Wren, and their successors. The walls, the doors, the windows, the chimney-pieces, the ceilings, and the staircases were alike affected.

Throughout the seventeenth century and well into the eighteenth the ancient methods of covering the walls prevailed; either with hangings or with panelling. The panels, however, became much larger; instead of being 12 or 15 in. wide, they were 3 ft. or more, and high in proportion. Hitherto they had usually been made in one sheet from floor to cornice; sometimes, however, a dado had been introduced; that is a range of panels near the floor, surmounted by a horizontal moulding which made the circuit of the room at the height of about 3 ft. from the floor, thus dividing the panelling into two unequal ranges, a low one below, and a lofty one above. This arrangement, instead of being the exception, now became the rule. The pilasters and cornices were more carefully and correctly designed—both those of the walls and those which embellished the

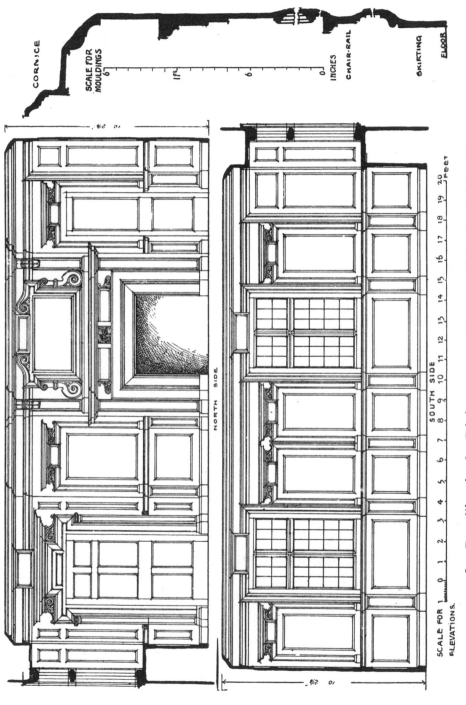

181. Panelling in the Dining-room at Thorney Hall, Cambridgeshire.

doorways. The broken pediment was introduced, and not infrequently the blank space left where the apex of the completed pediment would have been was filled with a cartouche of arms surrounded by foliage, and linked to the adjacent work by heavy swags of fruit and leaves (Fig. 195). All the detail was carefully designed, both as to its proportion, its purity of outline, and its suitable decoration with carving. Yet withal there was a freedom

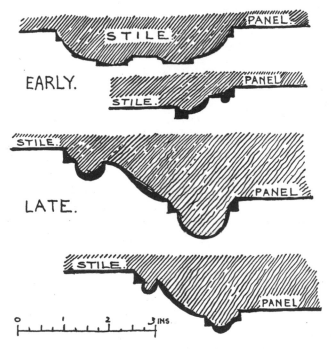

182. Typical Panel Mouldings of the Eighteenth Century.

and variety of treatment, a charming absence of too formal restraint, which were a legacy from the light-hearted and irresponsible methods of earlier days. At Thorney Hall in Cambridgeshire there is some excellent panelling of this kind (Fig. 181). It has been attributed to Inigo Jones, but from its close resemblance to the work at Thorpe Hall (Fig. 194), it may be more safely assigned to his pupil and successor, John Webb.

The mouldings of the panels became bolder ; instead of being narrow and kept within the face of the surrounding woodwork, they grew to 3 in. or more in width and projected considerably beyond the face ; the panel itself, instead of being recessed from the framing, not infrequently stood out in front of it (Fig. 182). The carving followed the same tendency ; instead of being flat in section, delicately modelled in conventional designs, and kept in subordination, adding an unobtrusive interest to the surrounding work, it asserted its independence, grew high in relief, assumed naturalistic forms, and challenged admiration on its own account. This is particularly noticeable in Grinling Gibbons' carving, which excites admiration by its life-like modelling and wonderful execution, yet often induces the feeling that it has been too eager to throw off the wholesome restraints of architectural treatment.

183. Boughton House, Northants
(*cir.* 1700).

View in State Apartments.

The large panels, the dado, the bold bolection mouldings are everywhere in evidence at Boughton House, where suites of rooms, opening one from the other, afford

184. House in Buckingham Street, Strand, London (1675).

long vistas through lofty doors (Fig. 183). There is an
excellent example in a house (now rebuilt) in Buckingham Street, near the Strand (Fig. 184), built about
1675 ; a house which was the residence of Peter the

185. Wilton House, Wiltshire.

Chimney-piece in the Single Cube Room (*cir.* 1648).

Great while he was studying at Deptford. By the
middle of the seventeenth century pilasters, as a means
of dividing wall-panelling into bays, had gone out of
fashion ; their place was sometimes taken, as at Wilton,

186. House in Hatton Garden, London. (Now destroyed.)

by carved drapery or flowers apparently hung on the
wall (Fig. 185); but even this attempt at grouping the
panels was subsequently relinquished, and the walls
became covered with nothing but the large panels,
crowned with a good cornice and relieved by the dado,
the windows, the doors, and the chimney-piece. This
simple but satisfactory treatment may be seen in number-
less houses of the time of Queen Anne and the early
Georges, where the panelling consists of nothing more

187. Treatment of One Side of a Room.

From Abraham Swan's "Designs in Architecture" (1757).

than slightly raised panels, surrounded by the plainest
of mouldings (Fig. 186). Later in the century the wood
panelling disappeared, and its place was taken by panels
sunk in the plaster of the walls, such as Abraham Swan
shows in his "Designs of Architecture" (Fig. 187), or by
the more elaborate plaster panels of the old War Office
(Fig. 188) attributed to Brettingham; or yet again by wall-
paper, such as is familiar to every one in the present day.

A considerable amount of attention was bestowed

188. Room in Old War Office, formerly Cumberland House, Pall Mall (1760-67).

(Now destroyed.) *Matthew Brettingham, Architect.*

upon doors and doorways, both external and internal. In Jacobean times external doorways were tolerably simple in themselves, and they were generally set back inside a porch, which was entered through a semicircular

189. Doorway at Cark Hall, Lancashire
(*cir.* 1623).

archway flanked by pilasters or columns carrying a frieze and cornice. Typical examples may be seen at Felbrigge Hall (Fig. 118) and Gayhurst (Fig. 126). This method was carried on during the first quarter of the seventeenth century. A later treatment occurs at Cark

190. Doorway formerly in Sherborne Lane, London.

At Godalming.

191. External Doorways.

At Petworth.

192. Manor House at Rothwell, Northamptonshire (*cir.* 1720).
Entrance Doorway.

Hall, Lancashire, where almost detached columns support a bold semicircular pediment which encloses a heavy wreath surrounding a coat of arms (Fig. 189).

In the eighteenth century a pediment over external doors became the established fashion, as a reference to the illustrations of the smaller houses (Figs. 171-173) will show. It rested either on a bold architrave, or on pilasters. If not a pediment, then there would be a bold hood generally fashioned internally in the similitude of a huge shell, such as may be seen at Burwash (Fig. 170), or, more at large, in a doorway which once stood in Sherborne Lane, London (Fig. 190). At first the pilasters and pediment were of stone, but later on they were made of wood protected from the weather by a covering of lead. Very charming features of this kind may be seen in almost any old country town; two illustrations, from Petworth and Godalming, are given in Fig. 191. It will be seen that each of them has an arrangement characteristic of the age in the shape of a fanlight over the door, a simple but really ingenious device for obtaining light where the

193. Raynham Hall, Norfolk (*cir.* 1636).

A Doorway.

entrance hall was not wide enough to allow of a window. The fanlight was always divided into comparatively small spaces by bars gracefully curved ; and it is surprising to what a variety of pleasing designs this fashion led.

194. Thorpe Hall, Northamptonshire (*cir.* 1656).

Doorway and Panelling.

Much fancy was displayed in the embellishment of doorways long after windows had become mere oblong apertures relieved only by stout crossbars. Even when the bulk of the windows were thus plain, a central feature was sometimes contrived by adopting a special treatment of the window over the door, as in the case of the manor house at Rothwell (Fig. 192).

Internal doorways in Jacobean times had frequently been lavishly ornamented, and the desire to achieve a handsome result had occasionally led to an extraordinary elaboration. In this respect, as in others, the cultivated taste of trained architects, such as Inigo Jones and Webb, led to a more sober and carefully calculated result. This may be seen at Raynham Park (Fig. 193) by Jones, and at Thorpe Hall (Fig. 194) by Webb, where there is a delightful mixture of freedom and austerity. Then came Wren with his massive and masculine hand, of which the influence, although probably not immediate and direct, is visible in the doorways at Combe Abbey (Fig. 195) and Love Lane (Fig. 210).

A type of general treatment became firmly established. The very large panels of the end of the seventeenth century, such as those adopted at Love Lane, gave place to smaller. Instead of two, doors had six or even more panels. They were surrounded by a bold architrave, and surmounted by an overdoor consisting of frieze and cornice, as may be seen in the example from Hatton Garden (Fig. 186); from the book of Abraham Swan (Fig. 187); from the old War Office (Fig. 188); or from the later houses shown in Fig. 196. All the component parts of the design—the architrave, the frieze, the cornice—lent themselves to enrichment by carving. But this was generally applied with discretion, and with a well-regulated wish to heighten the effect without overdoing it. The carving changed in character with the lapse of years. In the early part of the century it retained the boldness imparted by Wren and Vanbrugh, but gradually its vigour gave way to the delicacy and refinement associated with the names of the brothers Adam, of which type an excellent example is shown from Sheen House (Fig. 196, *b*).

The same gradual changes which took place in the

195. Doorway at Combe Abbey (1686).
Probably designed by Captain Wynne.

design of doorways also characterise the treatment of chimney-pieces. The small detail and elaborate ornament of the Jacobean style gave way to a simpler and larger handling. Already towards the close of the Jacobean

196. Three Internal Doorways.

a. From a House in Whitehall Gardens (before 1727).
b. From Sheen House, Richmond.
c. From Cumberland House (Old War Office, 1760-67).

period much of the exuberant carving and fretwork of
earlier times had been dropped, and in its place simple
columns and moulded panels had been adopted. The
obvious division of a chimney-piece into two stages, one
surrounding the fireplace, and the other filling the
wall space above it—a division which is most easily
described by the rather hackneyed terms mantel and

197. Chimney-piece from Raynham Hall.

overmantel—became more emphasised than it had been.
Many of the chimney-pieces of the time of Elizabeth and
James are so largely designed, both in size and scale,
that they strike the beholder as one composition rather
than as two halves. With the simplification of the
detail, the two-fold character became more apparent.
The space above the fireplace was often panelled after

the same general fashion as the rest of the room, but
with some special treatment to emphasise its important
position.   The chimney-piece consequently became a
one-storey feature.   This is the case in the room at
Wilton (Fig. 185), and also in a minor degree at Raynham Hall (Fig. 197).   But concurrently with this
treatment went another, which, while adopting the
division of mantel and overmantel, kept them both in
complete harmony, and made one feature of them.
Good examples of this were to be found in the house
in Hatton Garden, now destroyed (Figs. 186, 198).   The
blank space in the overmantel in Fig. 186 was probably
occupied by a picture, for it was a frequent custom to
insert in the panel over the fireplace some agreeable but
unexciting subject, such as a flowerpiece or a landscape
diversified with architectural ruins ; something which
should inspire a mild interest by its harmonious colour
and peaceful rendering.   A typical chimney-piece of the
early eighteenth century is reproduced from an original
drawing by the architect James Gibbs in Fig. 199.
This was clearly meant to be completed by a picture.
Another example of a similar kind is that from a house
in Whitehall Gardens (Fig. 200), which closely resembles
one of Kent's designs.   Sometimes instead of a picture
a mirror was introduced in this position ; but as large
sheets of glass were not yet procurable, the mirrors were
made long and low, and not infrequently in three
divisions of which the middle one was circular headed.

The treatment adopted about the middle of the
century may be gathered from the illustration taken
from Swan's book (Fig. 187) ; while that of a few years
later is shown in the specimen from Lansdowne House
by the brothers Adam (Fig. 201).   Here it will be seen
that the chimney-piece is an isolated feature, not part of
a general scheme of architectural decoration, for the

198. Chimney-piece from a House in Hatton Garden,
London. (Now destroyed.)

walls are papered, and the only reminiscence of the more monumental treatment of past times is the dado-rail. It was before some such fireplace as this, but simpler and less ornate, that Cowper sat on a winter evening when he heard the post-boy's horn sounding along the "wearisome but needful length" of the country bridge, and called upon his companion to

> "Stir the fire, and close the shutters fast,
>   Let fall the curtains, wheel the sofa round,
>   And while the bubbling and loud hissing urn
>   Throws up a steamy column, and the cups
>   Which cheer but not inebriate, wait on each,
>   So let us welcome peaceful evening in."

Except that the urn and the shutters have gone out of fashion, the picture might have been drawn in the present day, so far have we travelled from the central hearth of the Gothic hall. The stirring of the fire is a touch that reminds us of the disappearance of the open hearth, and the adoption of the fire-grate in its stead—a change which had occurred some sixty or seventy years before Cowper published his "Winter Evening" in 1785. No exact date can be assigned to the alteration, just as no exact date can be given to the practice of papering walls instead of panelling them or hanging them with tapestry. But in an inventory of two country houses belonging to a director of the South Sea Company, made in 1720, it is obvious that although grates were already in use the open hearth was still prevalent. Many of the rooms had fire-dogs, shovels, and tongs, but no poker; while others had a grate, shovel, tongs, and poker, but no fire-dogs. It is the dogs which were essential to the open hearth in order to keep the logs of wood in position, for wood was the fuel of the ancient fire; and it is the poker which was essential to the grate in order to break the coal, and

199. Chimney-piece designed by James Gibbs.

From an Original Drawing by the Architect.

coal was the fuel of the modern fire. The intermediate step was the dog-grate, which was in its essence a fire-basket holding coal, and placed in the old, large, open recesses. This expedient, however, was not entirely successful. The huge flues of the old days did not draw away the smoke from the small coal fires adequately; coal smoke is far more pungent and disagreeable than wood smoke; and therefore the next step was to increase the draught by combining with the grate a shield which should close the large opening of the open hearth, or by building it up with brickwork. The result was the first ancestor of the modern grate.

Just as the small panels of Jacobean woodwork gave way to the large panels of Wilton House and Boughton, so were the busy ceilings of the early seventeenth century gradually superseded by a more massive treatment. The older treatment survived in remote places till half-way through the century, and a plaster frieze of 1649, from Coles Farm, near Box in Wiltshire (Figs. 202, 203), shows how the old forms lingered on, although losing some of their vitality. The pattern in these busy ceilings covered the whole area, and the ground of the area was unbroken except by the pattern; any constructional beams that were required were concealed. But in course of time the beams asserted themselves, and were so arranged, with the addition of heavy ribs forming circular, oval, or octagonal panels, as to divide the area into several large spaces, thus breaking it up into deeply recessed divisions. The ornament, instead of being spread over the whole ceiling equally, was concentrated on and near the beams and ribs. The whole character of the ceiling was altered: instead of being a large, evenly fretted surface, it was broken up into several massive bays, which gave it a heavier and more monumental appearance. As in the wood-carving so in the

200. Chimney-piece in a House in Whitehall Gardens,
London (before 1727).

This chimney-piece closely resembles one in Kent's " Designs of
Inigo Jones," plate 63.

201. Chimney-piece from Lansdowne House, London (*cir.* 1765).

plasterwork, much greater relief was aimed at, and in some of the finest ceilings of the time of William and Mary much of the work is so detached as to require a framework of wire for its foundation. This large way of handling the ceiling prevailed throughout the latter

202. Plaster Frieze at Coles Farm, Box, Wiltshire (1649).

half of the seventeenth century, and is exemplified by the work at Thorpe Hall (Fig. 204), designed by Webb, the house in Buckingham Street (Fig. 184), and a house in Warwick Square in the city, once the home of a

203. Plaster Frieze at Coles Farm, Box.

wealthy merchant (Fig. 206). It survived in occasional examples till towards the close of the eighteenth century. Ware held it to be sufficiently in vogue to justify him in giving instructions as to the treatment of ceilings, and the design in Fig. 205 gives an excellent idea of the

204. Ceiling from Thorpe Hall, Northamptonshire (*cir.* 1656).

205. Ceiling designed by Isaac Ware.

system and of the contrast it presents to Jacobean
methods.   An example of yet later date is in a room
at the old War Office (Fig. 188), but here the main lines
are unconstructional in their shape : the subsidiary ornament is of the delicate type associated with the last
quarter of the eighteenth century.

206. Ceiling from a House in Warwick Square in the City
of London (*cir.* 1707).

Concurrently with the massive treatment just described, the eighteenth century saw a reversion to the
old idea of treating the ceiling as one large flat surface
and covering it with ornament in low relief.   A specimen

207. Room in a House in Whitehall Gardens, London, showing Flat Treatment of Ceiling (late 18th cent.).

of this type is seen in the house in Whitehall Gardens
(Fig. 207). The relief is very low, and the ornament is
of the discursive rococo type, wanting in an easily
intelligible *motif*. In equally low relief were the ceilings
designed by the brothers Adam, but their forms were
intelligible, and the modelling was full of delicacy and
refinement. A characteristic example of their work is
that from a house in Mansfield Street, London (Fig. 208).
In a great number of houses, especially the ordinary
unimportant house, the ceilings throughout the eighteenth
century were quite plain. The rooms depended for
their interest upon the panelling, the chimney-piece, and
the well-moulded cornice, which not infrequently was
carried along the ceiling beams, introduced in order to
lessen the depth of the floor-joists by shortening their
bearings to 7 or 8 ft.

An entirely different kind of ceiling, which had a
vogue of some fifty years, must not be overlooked. It
belongs perhaps less to the domain of architecture than
to that of painting, namely the painted ceilings associated
with the names of Verrio and Laguerre. Verrio was
brought over to England by Charles II., and he died
in 1707. Laguerre, whom he employed, and who carried
on the style after Verrio's death, lived till 1721. With
him the interest ceased, although Sir James Thornhill
went on painting ceilings for another dozen years. It
is only in great houses or public buildings that this
phase of decoration is to be found. The ceiling was
regarded as a vast canvas, and certainly no previous
painter had enjoyed so wide a field for the display of
his conceptions. As a rule both Verrio and Laguerre
succeeded in avoiding the weighting of their ceilings
with too ponderous matter. Their favourite subjects
were gods and goddesses seated upon clouds, and some
very clever drawing and painting they produced. Their

208. A Drawing-room in Mansfield Street, London.

R. & J. Adam, Architects.

work cannot well be compared with that of masters working under the ordinary conditions of a movable canvas, controllable light, and a vertical position for manual execution. Were their masterpieces more easily studied than by looking upwards at a ceiling, they would probably be held in higher esteem. Some idea

209. Painted Ceiling from Boughton House, Northampton-shire (attributed to Verrio, *cir.* 1700).

of the effect of this method of decoration may be gathered from Fig. 209, which gives part of a ceiling in Boughton House, attributed to Verrio. The dark cornice on the left is actually the soffit of the modelled plasterwork; everything else, including the shallow balustrade, is painted on the flat ceiling.

Staircases seem to have been an exception to that general tendency to increase the scale of detail which is apparent in work of the late seventeenth and eighteenth centuries. One of the characteristics of Jacobean staircases is the massiveness of their component parts, the newels, the balusters, the handrail, the string ; even the steps themselves were sometimes made of solid blocks of wood. The newels were carried up well above the handrail, and fashioned into finials, sometimes heavily moulded, sometimes made into a pedestal for a figure— a heraldic animal, a boy playing an instrument, a warrior or what not. The " string " which supported the ends of the steps was always stout and solid. Much of this early treatment was carried on till the end of the seventeenth century, as may be seen by referring to the illustration from a house in Love Lane (Fig. 210) traditionally associated with Wren. Here all the parts are as massive as of old, although the turned portions of the balusters are inclined to be thin. The most significant change is to be found in the newels, which are not carried up into a finial, but are furnished with a cap by mitring the mouldings of the handrail round them. Once this fashion was established, it held the field until newels were dis-pensed with in the later part of the eighteenth century, and the handrail wound in one continuous length from the bottom to the top of the staircase.

A passing phase of treatment, associated with the later half of the seventeenth century, is the carved floriated balustrade, such as is to be seen at Sudbury House in Derbyshire (Fig. 211). This is generally combined with massive newels, handrail, and string ; indeed, it could hardly be otherwise, for the carved foliage required a fair thickness of wood, and as the carving was almost necessarily made in straight lengths, there had to be newels to receive it. It is not a very

210. Staircase in a House in Love Lane, London (now destroyed).

(Late 17th cent.)

common form of treatment and is usually confined to large houses where expense was not a primary consideration. The same illustration affords good examples of plasterwork in the ceiling, and of woodwork in the doors. It will be seen how much larger in scale is this work than the work of the beginning of the seventeenth century.

With the eighteenth century the treatment of staircases grew more dainty. The handrail, newels, and balusters lessened in size; the outer string disappeared and the balusters rested on the ends of the steps themselves. The whole effect became lighter. In Austin Friars, London, there was a house of the date of 1704 (now destroyed) which had a fine staircase, illustrated in Fig. 212, where these changes are apparent. It will be seen also that the handrail is ramped, that is, curved upwards at each turn in the staircase in order to attain the proper level for being mitred round the top of the newel. In earlier work, it would have been carried in a straight line till it stopped against the newel, but as the newels are here twisted, there is no plain surface to receive it, and accordingly ramping becomes a necessity. The twisting of the balusters was a common device, more common than that of twisting the newels.

Occasionally the treads and risers were themselves ornamented, the treads being inlaid with various patterns, and the risers being panelled. There is a fine example of this treatment at the Hall at Glastonbury in Somerset,* of the date of 1726 (Fig. 213). The inlay is of mahogany and a light wood let into the oak of the treads. The first quarter-landing contains a panel with a monogram and date. It is obvious that no carpets were con-

---

* The residence of the Misses Baily, who have kindly allowed the staircase to be drawn.

211. Staircase from Sudbury Hall, Derbyshire.

212. Staircase from a House in Austin Friars, London, 1704.
(Now destroyed.)

templated for such staircases as these.   The newels and balusters in this instance are slightly carved as well as turned ; and the bracket at the end of each step is also carved, thus helping considerably towards the general richness of effect.

Later in the eighteenth century skill in the construction of staircases developed still further.   It seems a comparatively simple matter to build one in short straight flights with a stout string to carry the steps at either end of them.   It is rather less simple to cut away the outer string so as to let the ends of the steps project as in Figs. 212 and 213 ; the difficulty, however, is minimised by keeping the flights straight.   But it required greater skill, both in setting out and in construction, to depart from straight flights altogether, and to contrive a staircase in one continuous elliptical sweep from floor to floor.   One of the earliest examples of this method of design, of about 1700, is at Drayton House in Northamptonshire, but it became quite fashionable in the middle of the eighteenth century, and many specimens still survive in large houses in the Bloomsbury district of London, some in stone and some in wood.

The changes that took place in the length of the flights of staircases are not without interest.   In mediæval times, when staircases were of the corkscrew type, landings were sparsely provided, and in the nature of things they were small at the best—anything large would not only have interrupted the continuous spiral of ascent, but would have interfered with the already scanty headroom.   With the introduction of the wood staircases of the late sixteenth century, a complete change took place. They were made of ample width, and in straight, short flights, seldom of more than six or eight steps ; then came a quarter-landing, then another flight at right angles.   These short flights remained in fashion nearly

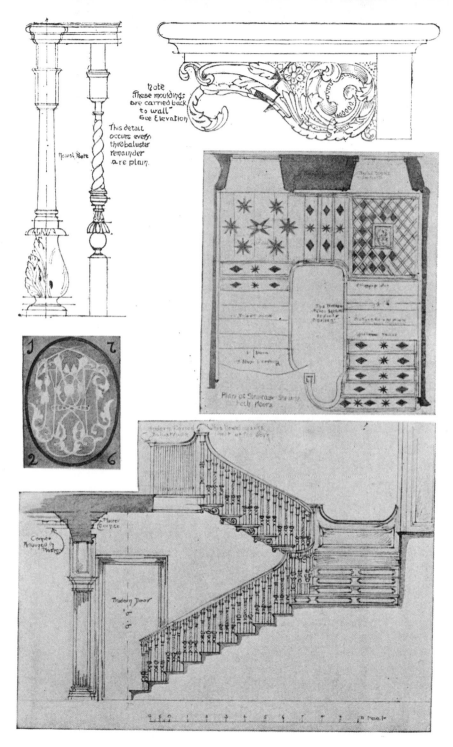

213. Staircase at the Hall, Glastonbury, Somerset (1726).

The dated inlaid panel is seen in the plan in the centre of the square
landing at the top of the first flight.

down to the eighteenth century.   Occasionally winders had been employed, but not in the finest examples. With the eighteenth century the flights increased in length, containing twelve, sixteen, or even more steps : winders were more frequently used.   Finally came the

214. Staircase in Baddow House, Essex.

elliptical staircase, sweeping from floor to floor in one flight without any landings, and consisting wholly of winders, although as the radius of the sweep was longer, they none of them were narrowed to an actual point. The general effect, which is not altogether happy, may

be gathered from Fig. 214. The balustrade here is of
iron, rather meagre in design, as such things had now
become ; the early years of the century had produced
some excellent specimens of iron stair-balustrades ; but
they were not of frequent occurrence, the usual material
being wood.

By the end of the eighteenth century the ordinary
methods of house design had become almost devoid of
interest ; the story of the growth of the English house
must therefore perforce end on a low note. The stream
of development had been fairly continuous up to then,
thenceforward it was to be diffused in various channels,
all of which derived their character from the past. The
Italian Renaissance had been the main source of inspiration, but soon the buildings of Greece were to furnish
ideas. After them came the Gothic revival ; the battle
of the styles ; the eclecticism of the nineteenth century ;
the negation of all style adopted by the speculative
builder, only one degree better than his vulgarisation of
all styles as he became aware of their existence. From
this Slough of Despond we seem now to be happily
emerging, and we shall do so the more certainly in proportion as we add to knowledge, thought, and common-
sense.

From the foregoing pages it is hoped that some
slight knowledge may be obtained ; but the dry bones
of the facts recorded must be clothed by the imagination
of the reader with their covering of flesh. " The cloud-
capp'd towers " of feudalism may, perhaps to his ear,
resound with the clash of armour ; "the gorgeous
palaces " of the Renaissance may echo with the melodious

notes of the Elizabethan singers or the stately cadence of a later age. Through the cross-bars of the portcullis his eye must detect the glint of steel and the glow of heraldry; across the latticed panes of the mullioned window he must watch for the passing of ruff, and cloak, and slashed hose; behind the glazed sashes he must picture the flowing wig, the patches, and the skirted coat. As the panorama of architecture unfolds itself before him he must people it with the forms of the savage Front-de-Bœuf, the valiant Hotspur, the courtly Sidney, glorious John, sententious Shandy, and the rest of the great band of immortals; and from the "worm-eaten holds of ragged stone," upon which his eye has lingered, he must for himself construct the homes that once they were.

CHRONOLOGICAL LIST OF CASTLES AND HOUSES.

THE list includes those mentioned in the text, together with a few others of note. It is not always possible to date houses accurately; a margin of a few years must usually be allowed. Where dates are given they either appear on the houses, or can be approximately ascertained. The Index to Illustrations shows which buildings are illustrated or referred to.

WILLIAM I.—1066-1087.
The White Tower, Tower of London

WILLIAM II.—1087-1100.
Colchester Castle, Essex
Westminster Hall, early parts

HENRY I.—1100-1135.
Rochester Castle, Kent, 1130 (*cir.*)
Castle Hedingham, Essex, 1130(*cir.*)
Norham Castle, Northumberland
Ludlow Castle, Shropshire, parts

STEPHEN—1135-1154.
Many castles subsequently destroyed

HENRY II.—1154-1189.
Dover Castle, Kent
Guildford Castle, Surrey
Jew's House, Lincoln
Castle Rising, Norfolk
Norham Castle, Northumberland, parts
Kenilworth Castle, Warwickshire, keep
Peak Castle, Derbyshire, keep, 1176
Oakham Castle, Rutland, 1180 (*cir.*)

RICHARD I.—1189-1199.
Haddon Hall, Derbyshire, early parts
Chacombe Priory, Northamptonshire, window

JOHN—1199-1216.
Conisborough Castle, Yorkshire

HENRY III.—1216-1272.
Stokesay, Shropshire, parts
Ludlow Castle, Shropshire, parts
Prebendal House, Nassington, Northamptonshire
Many additions and repairs to royal houses

EDWARD I.—1272-1307.
Little Wenham Hall, Suffolk
Longthorpe Tower, Northamptonshire
Acton Burnell, Shropshire, 1284 (*cir.*)
Stokesay Castle, Shropshire, parts; licence to crenellate, 19 Edw. I., 1291
Aydon Castle, Northumberland, licence, 33 Edw. I., 1305
Woodcroft Castle, Northamptonshire
Broughton Castle, Oxfordshire
Abingdon Abbey, Berkshire, parts

EDWARD II.—1307-1327.

Prudhoe Castle, Northumberland, oriel

Markenfield, Yorkshire, licence, 3 Edw. II., 1309

Yanwath, Westmorland, soon after 1322

Ightham Mote, Kent, parts

Leeds Castle, Kent

EDWARD III.—1327-1377.

Stanton Harcourt, Oxfordshire, licence, 1 Edw. III., 1327; early parts destroyed

Drayton House, Northamptonshire, licence, 2 Edw. III., 1328

Abingdon Abbey, Berkshire, parts; licence, 4 Edw. III., 1330

Lyddington, Rutland, licence, 10 Edw. III., 1336; existing parts, Henry VII.

Penshurst, Kent, licence, 15 Edw. III., 1341

Alnwick Castle, Northumberland

Haddon Hall, parts

Maxstoke Castle, Warwickshire, licence, 19 Edw. III., 1345

Northborough, Northamptonshire, licence, 20 Edw. III., 1346

Mayfield, Sussex, Bishop's Palace, 1349-66

Warwick Castle, licence, 45 Edw. III., 1371

RICHARD II.—1377-1399.

Amberley Castle, Sussex, licence, 1 Rich. II., 1377

Bodiam Castle, Sussex, licence, 9 Rich. II., 1386

Raby Castle, Durham

Baguley Hall, Cheshire

Kenilworth Castle, hall, &c., 1392 (cir.)

Westminster Hall, roof, &c.

Glastonbury Abbey, Somersetshire, kitchen

HENRY IV.—1399-1413.

HENRY V.—1413-1422.

HENRY VI.—1422-1461.

Hurstmonceux, Sussex, licence, 1 Henry VI., 1423

South Wingfield Manor House, Derbyshire, 1435-40 (cir.)

Tattershall Castle, Lincolnshire, 1440 (cir.)

Warkworth Castle, Northumberland, keep, 1435-40 (cir.)

Ewelme, Oxfordshire, almshouse and school, between 1437-48

Great Chalfield, Wiltshire

Norrington, Wiltshire

Little Sodbury, Gloucestershire

Sherborne Abbey, Dorset, fireplace

Church House, Salisbury, fireplace

Harringworth, Northamptonshire, chimney

EDWARD IV.—1461-1483.

Eltham Palace, Kent

Kirby Muxloe, Leicestershire, 1460 (cir.)

Hurstmonceux, parts

Crosby Hall, London

Stanton Harcourt, kitchen

Oxburgh Hall, Norfolk, 1482

EDWARD V.—1483.

RICHARD III.—1483-85.

HENRY VII.—1485-1509.

Cothele, Cornwall

Athelhampton, Dorsetshire

Lytes Carey, Somerset, Manor House

Lyddington, Bede House

Stanton Harcourt, parts

Cowdray House, Sussex

Ightham Mote, Kent, parts

Fawsley, Northamptonshire

Horham Hall, Essex, between 1502-20

East Barsham Hall, Norfolk

Brympton d'Evercy, Somerset

Eastington, Worcestershire

Abingdon Abbey, Guest-house

Crowhurst Place, Surrey

Lenham, Kent, doorway

Harrietsham, Kent, doorway

Glastonbury, doorway and windows

HENRY VIII.—1509-1547.

Layer Marney, Essex, 1500-25
Thornbury Castle, Gloucestershire, 1511-21
Bramhall Hall, Cheshire, parts, 1521 (*cir.*)
Hengrave Hall, Suffolk, 1525-38
Compton Winyates, Warwickshire, 1525 (*cir.*)
Sutton Place, Surrey, 1523-25
Clifton Maybank, Dorsetshire
Kirtling, Cambridgeshire, between 1530 and 1564
Lacock Abbey, Wiltshire, parts
Lacock, Angel Inn
Haddon Hall, parts, 1542
Moyns Park, Essex, early parts
Hampton Court, great hall
Cocklaw Tower, Northumberland
Sir Paul Pindar's House, London

EDWARD VI.—1547-1553.

Deene Park, Northamptonshire, parts
Longleat House, Wiltshire, early parts
Old Somerset House, London, 1546-56

MARY—1553-1558.

Burghley House, Northamptonshire, kitchen, great hall, &c., 1553 (*cir.*)
Park Hall, Oswestry, Shropshire, 1553-58
Dingley Hall, Northamptonshire, parts, 1558

ELIZABETH—1558-1603.

Moreton Old Hall, Cheshire, 1559
Buckhurst House, Sussex, 1560-65
Loseley, Surrey, 1562-68
Theobalds, Hertfordshire, 1564-88
Longleat House, Wiltshire, 1566-78
Gorhambury, Hertfordshire, 1568
Kirby, Northamptonshire, 1570-75
Deene Park, Northamptonshire, chimney-piece, 1571
Hardwick Hall, Derbyshire, 1576
Burghley House, courtyard, 1577-87
Montacute, Somerset (entrance porch earlier), 1580

Wollaton Hall, Nottinghamshire, 1580-88
Longford Castle, Wiltshire, 1580
Moyns Park, brick part, 1580 (*cir.*)
Holdenby, Northamptonshire, 1580-85
Corsham Court, Wiltshire, 1582
Barlborough Hall, Derbyshire, 1583
Cobham Hall, Kent, 1584-95
Wimbledon, Surrey, 1588
Beaufort House, Chelsea, 1590 (*cir.*)
Wakehurst Place, Sussex, 1590
Westwood Park, Worcestershire, 1590
Astley Hall, Lancashire
Powis Castle, Wales
Bramhall Hall, Cheshire, parts, 1592
Brome Hall, Suffolk
Herringstone, Dorsetshire
Wolveton, Dorsetshire
Parham, Sussex, 1593
Rushton Hall, Northamptonshire, 1595, parts
Doddington, Lincolnshire, 1595
Gayhurst, Buckinghamshire, 1597, parts
Condover Hall, Shropshire, 1598
Marton Hall, Cheshire
Burton Agnes, Yorkshire, 1602-10

JAMES I.—1603-1625.

Audley End, Essex, 1603-16
Chastleton, Oxfordshire, 1603 (*cir.*)
Knole, Kent, 1605
Bramshill, Hampshire, 1605-12
Charlton House, Wiltshire, 1607
Fountains Hall, Yorkshire, 1611
Hatfield House, Hertfordshire, 1612
Cranborne Manor House, Dorsetshire, parts, 1612
Bolsover Castle, Derbyshire, 1613
Crewe Hall, Cheshire, 1615-36
Aston Hall, Warwickshire, 1618-35
Blickling, Norfolk, 1619-20
Houghton Conquest, Bedfordshire, 1620 (*cir.*)
Quenby Hall, Leicestershire, 1602 (*cir.*)
Banqueting Hall, Whitehall, 1622
Apethorpe, Northamptonshire, parts, 1623-24

King's Lynn, chimney-piece at, 1623
Cark Hall, Lancashire, 1623 (*cir.*)
Stibbington Hall, Huntingdonshire, 1625
Felbrigge Hall, Norfolk
Heath Hall, Yorkshire
Derwent Hall, Derbyshire
Gayhurst, Buckinghamshire
Calgarth Old Hall, Cumberland
Pilton Manor House, Northampton-shire
Lyveden Old Building, Northamptonshire
Hall of Butchers' Guild, Hereford

CHARLES I.—1625-1649.

Rushton Hall, parts, 1627
Raynham Park, Norfolk, 1630-36
Stoke Park, Northamptonshire, 1630-36
Stanway, Gloucestershire, 1630 (*cir.*)
Kenyon Peel Old Hall, Lanca-shire, 1631
Wilton, Wiltshire
Swakeleys, Middlesex

COMMONWEALTH—1649-1660.

Sudbury Hall, Derbyshire
Coles Farm, Box, Wiltshire, 1649
Coleshill, Berkshire, 1650
Ashburnham House, Westminster, 1650-60
Thorney Hall, Cambridgeshire
Amesbury House, Wiltshire, 1654
Tyttenhanger, Hertfordshire, 1654
Thorpe Hall, Northamptonshire, 1656 (*cir.*)
Cold Overton, Leicestershire

CHARLES II.—1660-1684.

Hampstead Marshall, Berkshire, 1662
Ashdown House, Berkshire, 1665-66 (*cir.*)
The Vicarage, Burford, Oxfordshire, 1672
House in Buckingham Street, Strand, 1675
Groombridge Place, Kent
Chatsworth, Derbyshire, 1681

JAMES II.—1684-1688.

Newcastle House, Lincoln's Inn Fields, 1686
Combe Abbey, Warwickshire, 1686
Melton Constable, Norfolk, 1687

WILLIAM AND MARY—1688-1702.

Belton House, Lincolnshire, 1689
Hampton Court, parts
"Roppynden," Burwash, Sussex, 1699
Boughton House, Northampton-shire, 1700 (*cir.*)
Drayton House, parts and iron-work, 1700 (*cir.*)
House in Love Lane, London

ANNE—1702-1714.

House in Austin Friars, London, 1704
House in Warwick Square, London, 1707 (*cir.*)
Apple Dorecombe, Isle of Wight ("Vitruvius Britannicus"), 1710
Easton Neston, Northamptonshire, 1713
Kings Weston, Gloucestershire ("Vit. Brit."), 1713
Duncomb Park, Yorkshire ("Vit. Brit."), 1715
Fenton House, Hampstead
Castle Howard, Yorkshire, 1714

GEORGE I.—1714-1727.

Blenheim, Oxfordshire, 1715
Wanstead, Essex, 1719 (*cir.*)
Seaton Delaval, Northumberland, 1720
Moor Park, Hertfordshire, 1720
Stoneleigh Abbey, Warwickshire, 1720 (*cir.*)
Mereworth, Kent, 1722
Houghton, Norfolk, 1723
Glastonbury Hall, 1726
Villa at Chiswick, 1729
Rothwell Manor House, Northamp-tonshire
Rectory, Burford
House in Whitehall Gardens

Heale House, Middle Woodford, Wiltshire

House at Horsham, Sussex

Ironwork at Carshalton House, Surrey

Ironwork at Eaton Hall, Cheshire

GEORGE II.—1727-1760.

House in Hatton Garden

Woburn Abbey, Bedfordshire, 1747

Prior Park, Bath, 1750 (*cir.*)

Holkham Hall, Norfolk, 1754 (*cir.*)

GEORGE III.—1760-1820

Harewood House, Yorkshire, 1760

Cumberland House, 1760-67

Kedlestone, Derbyshire, 1761

Lansdowne House, 1765 (*cir.*)

House in Mansfield Street, London, 1770 (*cir.*)

House in St James's Square, London, 1772

Somerset House, Strand, 1776

Baddow House, Essex

House at Faversham, Kent

House at Colchester

GLOSSARY.

AISLE.—The wing of a church, at the side of the nave or choir.

ARABESQUE.—Ornamentation enriching flat surfaces.

ASHLAR.—Hewn or squared stone, as distinguished from that which is rough or unhewn.

BALL-FLOWER.—A mediæval ornament resembling a ball placed within a globular flower.

BASE.—The lower part of a pillar or column.

BATTLEMENT.—An indented parapet, often pierced for the discharge of arrows.

BOLECTION MOULDING.—A moulding (in joinery) which projects beyond the surface of the framework round a panel.

BOSS.—A projecting ornament placed at the intersection of the ribs of a ceiling or of vaulting.

BUTTRESS.—A projection from a wall to create additional strength or support.

CAP., abbrev. for CAPITAL.—The upper part or head of a pillar or column.

CHIMNEY-PIECE.—The architectural decoration surrounding a fire place.

COPING.—The covering course of a wall or parapet to protect it from the weather.

CORBEL.—A projecting stone to carry a weight.

CORNICE.—The horizontal moulded projection encircling a building, or the upper part of the walls of a room below the ceiling.

COUNTER-HAURIANT.—A heraldic term. Counter = reversed : hauriant = swimming vertically. Two fishes swimming vertically, facing each other, are counter-hauriant.

CRENELLATE.—To fortify with battlements.

CROCKET.—Projecting leaves or flowers placed on pinnacles, gables, or the mouldings of doors and windows, &c.

CROSS-BRACE.—An oblique wooden tie or support.

CUSP.—A projecting point in the arches of tracery.

DADO.—The architectural treatment of the lower part of the walls of a room.

DAÏS.—The raised part of the floor at the upper end of a hall.

DOG-GATE.—A gate placed across a staircase to prevent dogs from going into the upper rooms of a house.

DORMER.—A window in a roof.

ENTABLATURE.—A series of horizontal mouldings at the summit of a wall, or surmounting a row of columns. An entablature consists of three members. The lowest is a series of mouldings of slight projection, called the architrave. Above this is a vertical face, called the frieze; above this a series of widely projecting mouldings, called the cornice.

FINIAL.—The ornamental finish at the apex of a gable.

FIREPLACE.—A recess in a wall for the reception of a fire, furnished with a flue or vent for the escape of smoke.

FRIEZE.—The middle member of an entablature, *q.v.*

GABLE.—The pointed wall at the end of a roof.

GARDE-ROBE.—A latrine or privy.

GATEHOUSE.—A building surrounding the gate to the courtyard of a house.

HIPPED ROOF.—A roof of which all the sides are sloped, one of which does not abut against a gable.

JAMB.—The side of a doorway, window, or other aperture.

LABEL.—The outer projecting moulding, or drip-stone, over a door, window, or arch.

LANTERN.—A turret raised above a roof for the admission of light.

LOUVRE.—A turret raised above a roof for the escape of smoke.

MACHICOLATION.—The corbelling out of the parapet of a building, forming openings through which missiles could be discharged on the heads of an attacking force.

MAUNCH.—The heraldic term for a sleeve.

MINSTRELS' GALLERY.—The gallery formed above the screen of a hall, sometimes occupied by minstrels.

MITRE (in Joinery).—The line formed by a sharp change (at right angles or otherwise) in the direction of a moulding.

MOULDING.—The term applied to the contour, wrought into long hollows and projections, of the angles or edges of an architectural feature, such as a door, window, arch, panel, &c.

MULLION.—The vertical shaft or division between the lights of a window.

NAVE.—The central portion of a church westward of the choir or chancel.

NEWEL.—In a circular stone staircase, the central column round which the steps wind. In a wooden staircase, the stout posts which carry the handrail and the string supporting the stairs.

OGEE.—A compound curve, partly concave and partly convex.

OILLET.—A loophole for the discharge of arrows.

ORIEL.—A bay window on an upper floor, corbelled out from the wall below.

PANELLING.—A series of panels formed of boards whose edges are held in the groove of a thicker surrounding frame.

PARAPET.—The upper part of a wall carried above the springing of the roof. Where the roof was flat it formed a protection to those who used the roof for defence or other purposes.

PEDESTAL.—A substructure carrying a column or pilaster.

PEDIMENT.—The triangular or segmental space formed by the carrying up of a cornice over a door or window or in a gable, &c.

PEEL or PELE.—A fortified tower or stronghold forming a dwelling ; a term principally applied to the fortified houses of the North.

PIER.—A pillar or column ; also sometimes a flat buttress.

PILASTER.—A square pillar or column attached to a wall, usually of slight projection.

PITCH (of a Roof).—The slope.

PORTCULLIS.—A strong grating of timber which slid up and down in a groove, to protect the entrance of a castle or fortified house.

PRINCIPAL (Rafter).—A massive framing of wood which spans a building from wall to wall and carries the purlins.

PURLIN.—A stout piece of timber resting on the principals and carrying the common rafters.

QUATREFOIL (in Tracery).—A form composed of four segments of circles.

QUOINS.—The external angles of a building ; also the stones which form the angles.

RESPOND.—A half-column attached to a wall.

RIBS (Stone).—Narrow projecting stones which form the framework of vaulting.

SASH-WINDOW.—A window in two halves, one over the other, which slide up and down.

SCANTLING.—The dimensions of a piece of timber in breadth and thickness.

SCREENS.—The entrance passage formed at the end of a hall by the screen.

SHAFT.—A small column.

SOLAR.—The retiring or private room of the lord in early houses.

SPAN.—The width between the supports of an arch or roof.

SPANDREL.—The space between an arch and the horizontal feature above it.

SQUINCH.—An arch carried across the internal angle of a tower or building.

STOREY.—A horizontal division of a building containing rooms at one level.

STRING (of a Staircase).—The inclined piece of wood which carries the steps.

STRING-COURSE.—A narrow projecting horizontal line of stone or brickwork.

TRACERY.—The ornamental stonework of a Gothic window formed by ramifications of the mullions ; also decorations of a corresponding character applied to panels, &c.

TRANSOME.—The horizontal cross-bar of a casement window (as distinguished from a sash-window).

TRIFORIUM.—An upper storey over the aisle of a church, with arches opening into the nave or choir.

TYMPANUM.—The space enclosed between the flat head of a door or window and the surmounting arch.

UNDERCROFT.—A vaulted chamber underground.

VAULTING.—An arched roof or ceiling of stone or brick.

WINDERS (of a Staircase).—The steps sometimes formed where a staircase changes direction ; they are wide against the wall and are narrowed almost to a point against the newel or string.

A Brief List of Books recommended for the Study of The History of English Domestic Architecture.

ADDY (S. O.)—THE EVOLUTION OF THE ENGLISH HOUSE. Small 8vo. 1905.

TURNER (T. H.) AND PARKER (J. H.)—SOME ACCOUNT OF DOMESTIC ARCHITECTURE IN ENGLAND DURING THE MIDDLE AGES. 3 vols. in 4. 8vo. 1859-1877.

GARNER (T.) AND STRATTON (A.)—THE DOMESTIC ARCHITECTURE OF ENGLAND DURING THE TUDOR PERIOD. 3 parts. Folio. 1908-1909.

GOTCH (J. A.)—ARCHITECTURE OF THE RENAISSANCE IN ENGLAND. 2 vols. Folio. 1891-1894.

GOTCH (J. A.)—EARLY RENAISSANCE ARCHITECTURE IN ENGLAND. 8vo. 1901.

NASH (J.)—MANSIONS OF ENGLAND IN THE OLDEN TIME. 4 vols. Folio. 1839-1849 ; or Small Edition. 4 vols. 4to. 1869.

BELCHER (J.) AND MACARTNEY (M. E.)—LATER RENAISSANCE ARCHITECTURE IN ENGLAND. 2 vols. Folio. 1901.

BLOMFIELD (R. T.)—A HISTORY OF RENAISSANCE ARCHITECTURE IN ENGLAND. 2 vols. Imp. 8vo. 1897 ; and Abridged Edition. Small 8vo. 1900.

INDEX TO ILLUSTRATIONS.

*NOTE.—J. A. G. stands for J. Alfred Gotch ; W. T. for William Twopeny ;
p. = photograph ; d. = drawing.*

INDEX TO TEXT.
